"The television movie, *The Last Dance,* was tender and touching, but Todd Copes's book *The Shift,* upon which the film was based, was more stirring than the movie.

Now Todd has done it again. Once you pick up *So Much for Christmas* you won't put it down until you've made it to the end. Then you'll sit there wishing for more. No story is as thrilling to me as a family who has drifted apart coming back together. The way this happens in this short novel is as surprising as it is heart-warming."

— *George Durrant, author*

"This book is a fun, quick read that touches the heart. I cried at the tenderness of a mother's love for her children, and I rejoiced at the strengthening ties of understanding among the children. How we treat other people in our families does make a difference."

— *Joan Fairbanks Reynolds,*
Supervisor of Assessment,
Salt Lake City School District

SO MUCH FOR
Christmas

Rosemary!
May the spirit of
the holiday season be
a part of your whole
year.

SO MUCH FOR

Christmas

BY

TODD F. COPE

BONNEVILLE BOOKS™

Springville, Utah

ISBN: 1-55517-710-7
e.1

Published by CFI
An imprint of Cedar Fort Inc.
www.cedarfort.com
Distributed by:

Cover design by Nicole Cunningham
Cover design © 2003 by Lyle Mortimer
Printed in the United States of America
10 9 8 7 6 5 4 3 2 1
Printed on acid-free paper

Library of Congress Cataloging-in-Publication Data

Cope, Todd F.
  So much for Christmas / by Todd F. Cope.
        p. cm.
  ISBN 1-55517-710-7 (pbk. : alk. paper)
1.   Maternal deprivation--Fiction. 2.   Mother and child--Fiction. 3.
Puerto Rico--Fiction. 4.   Children--Fiction. 5.   Robbery--Fiction. I.
Title.

  PS3603.O682723S6 2003
  813'.6--dc21

                        2003013329

DEDICATION

To my mother Florence, who gave me the idea for the outcome of the story and whose life is reflected in all that is good in Martha Cooper.

To my wife Denise and our four children who have been patient through all of my frustration, excitement and every other emotion that has been part of the writing process.

To Dave Griffin for all his vital help with the research that made Puerto Rico come to life. To the many friends and family members who took the time to read the manuscript and give suggestions for changes and improvements.

CHAPTER ONE

"I still don't think it's right, Martha," Sarah said as she closed the trunk of her yellow 1973 Cadillac. "Your children should be taking you to the airport."

Martha just chuckled and shook her head. Sarah seemed to be begging for a repeat of the discussion they had finished less than twenty minutes earlier. "You're right, Sarah," Martha patronized, hoping to end the taunting.

Though Martha had known Sarah for more than fifteen years, they had only been close friends for a short time. Both of them had lost their husbands to an untimely death three years before. That seemed to be about the only thing they had in common. Yet somehow it drew them together in some sort of timeless bond.

"Of course I'm right," Sarah said, "your children never seem to be around when you need them."

"You know that's not true," Martha defensively returned. "James was planning on taking me until he was called out of town on business. Anyway, we just went over this." Angry with herself for being pulled back into the interminable conversation, Martha walked to the front of the car and got in.

Grinning like a schoolgirl who had just manipulated a boy into carrying her books, Sarah climbed behind the steering wheel and continued. "So if James couldn't make it, why didn't one of the others offer?"

Martha opened her mouth to speak, but was interrupted.

"Of course, there's no way Thomas could offer." Sarah started the car and backed out of the driveway.

"Sarah, we've been through this—twice. Now, could we please talk about something else?" Martha turned and looked out the window at the freshly fallen snow as they drove out of town. She knew it would be too much to expect Sarah not to be raving about something for the entire forty-minute drive to the airport, but hoped she could at least change the subject.

"Well, it's just a good thing I was available, or you would have had to call a taxi." Sarah continued with newfound enthusiasm. "Do you know what a taxi ride to the airport would have cost? And it would have been dangerous too. A woman should never ride alone in a taxi. You don't have to take a taxi in San Juan do you?"

"No," Martha responded, "the cruise company provides a shuttle from the airport."

"You know if you had just waited until next year, I would have been able to go on this cruise with you. It would have been much more fun and a lot safer," Sarah said sincerely.

"Maybe we can still go together sometime, but I've been planning this since before Paul died. I need to do this and I can take care of myself," Martha said unconvincingly. This was the first time she had traveled on her own. It was her opportunity to prove her independence and she was determined to do it.

Sarah spent the rest of the drive giving travel and safety tips to Martha, who patiently endured. As they pulled up to the curb at the airport terminal, Sarah mumbled something about young people having no respect for seniors in Cadillacs. She went to the back of the car and opened the trunk so Martha could get her bags.

"I think I can make it from here," Martha said.

"You're sure one of your kids will be here to pick you up next week?" Sarah asked. "It would be a shame for them to leave you abandoned on Christmas Eve."

"Yes, I'm sure," Martha replied confidently. "Now don't you worry about me, I'll be just fine."

Sarah put her arms around Martha. "Remember what I said; don't keep your money or your credit card in your purse."

"Thank you, I'll be fine," Martha assured.

"Merry Christmas, Martha."

"Thank you Sarah, and Merry Christmas to you too," Martha returned. She waved as Sarah got into her car and pulled away from the curb.

Placing the strap of her small bag over one shoulder and her purse on the other, Martha grasped the handle of her bigger suitcase and moved toward the huge building looming in front of her. It had been years since she had been inside the airport, and it seemed larger than she had remembered. Suddenly she recalled how she had felt on her first day of school: frightened by the prospects of what lay ahead, but determined to succeed. "At least I'm not crying this time," she said to herself as she made her way to the queue at the check-in counter.

Several people were in line ahead of her, so Martha put her bags on the shiny tile floor. She removed her gloves and put them in her coat pockets, then opened her spacious purse and rummaged through its contents until she found her ticket. Clutching it to her chest, she smiled with satisfaction. This was the cruise she and Paul were planning to take in celebration of their thirty-fifth wedding anniversary. It would have been easy to forget about the trip after Paul's sudden heart attack, but deep inside, she knew that he would have wanted her to go.

In spite of the occasional interruption for announcements, Martha was grateful for the soft Christmas music that was playing over the airport sound system and acting as a much-needed distraction.

As she advanced in line, Martha pushed her bags across the floor with her foot. After what seemed like hours, it was finally her turn to approach the counter. Scooting her luggage to the stainless steel scale, she directed her questioning eyes to the person behind the counter.

"Just place those bags on the scale," the agent said pointing to her right. Her friendly tone and understanding smile immediately put Martha at ease. "Traveling alone?" she continued as she took Martha's ticket and stamped it.

"Yes I am," Martha replied. "It's my first cruise."

"You be careful ma'am, especially in San Juan," the young woman cautioned.

Martha's increasing sense of comfort suddenly edged back towards anxiety. "What do you mean?" she asked.

"Oh, I don't mean to scare you, it's just that you're going to a strange place on your own," she responded.

"You'll be just fine as long as you stay with your tour group."

Martha didn't respond, but nodded and shook her head appropriately to all the requisite questions that followed.

The ticket agent tore the boarding pass from the rest of the ticket and placed it in the jacket containing Martha's itinerary. "Your plane leaves from gate C-13," she said, handing it to Martha. "You'll be changing planes in Atlanta, but your luggage will go straight through to San Juan. You have the boarding pass for both flights, so you can go directly to the appropriate gate in Atlanta. Any questions?"

"How will I find my new plane in Atlanta?" Martha asked.

"There will be people to help you find your way when you arrive," the young women responded. "Enjoy your trip."

"Thank you, I will," Martha replied, "and Merry Christmas."

The woman smiled, "Merry Christmas, Ma'am."

After watching the young lady push her bags onto the conveyor belt that led to who-knows-where, Martha placed her purse back over her shoulder. "I hope my luggage ends up the same place I do," she said to no one in particular as she made her way to the escalators.

On the second level, Martha was fascinated by all of the security devices she was required to pass through. She was beginning to feel more secure in her surroundings and was almost disappointed when she didn't cause the metal detector to alarm. The officer operating the

X-ray machine smiled at Martha as she retrieved her handbag. Everyone seems so friendly, she thought. Confidently she hurried to the moving sidewalks that stretched down the long corridor leading to her gate.

As far as she could see, there were planes of various sizes lined up on the tarmac outside the glassed-in hallway. Her heart began to race with anticipation as she was conveyed toward gate C-13.

Martha nearly lost her balance as she stepped from the moving sidewalk onto the stationary floor of the crowded corridor. In the distance she could see the blue and white sign marking her departure point. She made her way through the throng of holiday travelers to the gate.

Unable to find an unoccupied seat, Martha positioned herself near the window overlooking what she assumed was the aircraft that would soon be taking her to Atlanta. She had never flown in such a large plane. In fact, the only time she had ever flown was as a child. She and her mother had traveled a few hundred miles to see her aunt and a new cousin. Unlike the Boeing 727 she was now viewing, her earlier trip was on a small commuter plane with room for about twenty passengers. She remembered the noise from the two prop engines and wondered if jet engines were as loud.

The first call to begin boarding the plane came across the intercom. Martha took the boarding pass from her purse and began looking for her seat number. 19C, an aisle seat, or so she had been told. She stood nervously shifting her weight from one foot to the other until it was time for her go.

When her turn came, Martha joined the others in line. She smiled as she showed her boarding pass to the young man in his official-looking blue coat with gold stripes on the sleeves. Moving up the gangway with the other passengers, she sensed an almost eerie change. The air became musty and sounds muted. She felt almost claustrophobic in the dim light. Taking deeper breaths, she moved around a bend and was relieved to see the airplane door in front of her.

Martha relaxed as she stepped onto the plane. The interior was bright and the air, though still somewhat musty, was moving to create a slight breeze. She was grateful for the help of the flight attendants, who directed her to her seat and made sure she was settled.

Feeling quite at ease and determined to enjoy the trip, Martha began looking around at all the other passengers. It was obvious that this would be a full flight. She should have no difficulty finding someone to talk to.

When the flight attendants began giving their instructions, Martha listened intently. She found the appropriate leaflet in the seat pocket and followed along as they talked about the flotation devices and oxygen masks. She located the nearest exit and secured her seat belt. Martha noted that the young man seated next to her had been reading during the entire lecture and the man next to him seemed to be sleeping.

"You must fly a lot," Martha said, hoping to start a conversation.

"Yes," the man muttered without lifting his eyes from the newspaper in his hands.

He was dressed in a dark gray business suit and Martha guessed he was probably about the age of her older children. "Business or pleasure?" she asked.

"Uh, business mostly," he said, still reading.

"This is my first flight. Well, sort of," Martha said.

Realizing that he would not be able to escape a conversation with his neighbor, the man lifted his head and peered over the top of the paper. "Sort of your first flight?" he inquired.

"It's my first flight in many years and my very first in a jet," Martha explained.

Placing the newspaper in his lap, the man extended his right hand towards Martha. "Joseph Watkins," he said.

"Pleased to meet you Joseph Watkins. I'm Martha Cooper," she said grasping his large hand with her slender fingers.

"If you're like me, you'll enjoy the flight, especially take-off and landing," Joseph said. "The rest is quite boring unless you hit turbulence."

"Do you think we will?" Martha asked.

"Well, I make this flight about once a month and only remember a few times that rough air made it unpleasant."

"Sounds like the odds are in our favor," Martha said.

Joseph and Martha continued their exchange as the plane taxied down the runway and took-off for a cruising altitude of 29,000 feet. The dull roar of the engines seemed to help muffle everything that was not part of their friendly conversation.

Martha felt fortunate to be sitting next to someone as kind as Joseph.

"So what takes you to Atlanta?" Joseph asked as he folded his newspaper and tucked it down the side of his seat between his leg and the armrest.

"My wedding anniversary. I'm taking a cruise," Martha replied.

"*I'm* taking a cruise? For *my* anniversary?" Joseph looked perplexed. "Sounds like a fun way to spend Christmas, but don't couples usually celebrate these kinds of things together?"

Martha chuckled. "I suppose that did sound strange. Actually, my husband died a few years ago. This cruise was planned to celebrate our 35th wedding anniversary. After he was gone, I decided not to go, but then some-thing told me Paul would still want me to make the trip. So I saved my money and here I am. I'm a couple of years late, but I'm doing it."

"I'm sorry, I didn't mean to get so personal," Joseph apologized.

"No, you're fine. If I didn't want you to know, I wouldn't have told you. Anyway, I love talking about my Paul." Martha folded her arms across her chest and stared at the ceiling as she continued. "It may seem morbid to some, but I don't mind talking about his death because that always leads to thoughts of his life. He was a good man — a good husband and provider and a loving father. I miss seeing him, but I feel like he's still with me."

"Sounds like he was a great guy," Joseph said. Sensing that Martha wanted to say more, he continued his line of questioning. "So how did you and Paul meet?"

"It's not really that exciting," Martha admitted, "but if you're sure you want to hear it."

"I'm sure," Joseph assured.

Martha shrugged and began with little hesitation. "I was hiking with some college friends in the hills behind the stadium. We were looking for an abandoned cabin we'd been told about. When we found it, we decided it would be a good place to eat our picnic lunch. We had just started eating when Paul and his friends came along and had the same idea." Martha smiled and winked at Joseph. "Of course it was the cabin they were interested in, not the three young girls who also happened to be there."

"I'm sure you're right," Joseph said returning the wink.

"This cabin was a popular hiking destination with the college crowd. I guess it was tradition that dictated the need for all visitors to attempt the rock challenge. The idea was to stand in front of the cabin and throw a rock all the way to the back through two window openings. I'm not sure what it meant if you succeeded, but I suppose at that age it didn't matter."

Still lost in thought, Martha was startled by a tap on her shoulder.

She looked over at Joseph who was pointing toward the aisle. "She'd like to know if you want something to drink," he said.

Martha turned to her right and smiled sheepishly. "I'm sorry, I didn't mean to ignore you," she said to the young woman. "I'll have a ginger ale."

The hostess responded with a genuine smile. She poured the soda into a clear glass with round, hollow chunks of ice and handed it to Martha. "And you sir?" she asked looking at Joseph.

"I'll have the same, thank you," Joseph responded.

"I hope you're enjoying the flight," the young woman said instinctively while pouring a second drink from the same can and placing it on the tray-table in front of Joseph. "I don't think I'll disturb him," she whispered, pointing at the man still sleeping in the window seat. Handing a bag of pretzels and a paper napkin to both Martha and Joseph, she proceeded up the aisle with her cart.

"I can tell she enjoys her job," Martha said.

"I'm sure she does," Joseph responded almost mindlessly. "You were telling me about the cabin and the rock challenge."

"Oh yes, the rock challenge." Martha took a sip of her drink before continuing. "My friends and I had each made several unsuccessful attempts at throwing a rock all the way through the cabin interior. With each attempt, we could hear Paul and his buddies from the other side. They were making all kinds of sarcastic comments about our throwing abilities. We yelled back that we wanted to see if they could do any better." Martha shook her head. "To our surprise, they did. Each one in turn hurled a rock through the window on their side and it ended up in front of us."

"Now that would be annoying," Joseph said with a chuckle. "And how did you respond?"

"Like any girl with a lick of pride would. I picked up

a rock and moved toward the window. I could see Paul on the other side. 'You'd better move,' I yelled. 'You couldn't hit the broad side of a barn if it jumped out in front of you,' he taunted."

Martha closed her hand as if holding something in it and raised it over her head.

Joseph was enthralled by the story and entertained by how worked-up Martha was getting. He had to tilt his head to the side to avoid being hit in the face by Martha's closed fist.

Completely unaware of Joseph's defensive move, Martha continued. "I closed my eyes and threw as hard as I could." As she spoke, her hand lunged forward hitting Joseph's tray table and knocking his glass.

Joseph grabbed his napkin and began wiping up the spilled drink as Martha gasped with embarrassment. "Well, go on," Joseph said, apparently undisturbed.

Martha smiled as she continued. "That rock went straight through both windows and hit Paul right in the forehead."

"What did he say about that?" Joseph inquired.

"Ouch!" was Martha's smug reply.

CHAPTER TWO

"Sounds like your relationship had a rocky beginning," Joseph said with a smile.

Martha appeared confused and then began to laugh. Joseph soon followed suit. Their laughter increased until neither was able to stop.

"Excuse me! Do you mind?" The anger could almost be felt as the large man sitting by the window glared at Martha. He squinted as he tried to adjust his eyes to the light. One side of his flushed face bore the imprint of the airplane paneling where his head had been resting. The small amount of fiery red hair that formed a semicircle around his head was soaked with perspiration and pointing in every direction.

"We're sorry," Martha responded sincerely. "We didn't mean to wake you."

Joseph stopped laughing and turned to face the man but on seeing his appearance, quickly turned back toward Martha. He put his hand over his mouth and pinched his nose with his thumb and forefinger.

Joseph's obvious attempt to stifle his chuckling made Martha blush. "Joseph, stop that," she whispered through the corner of her closed mouth while trying to maintain a smile.

Unable to contain himself any longer, Joseph burst into uncontrolled laughter. "I'm sorry," he mouthed to

Martha. "I'm sorry," he repeated to his angry neighbor between gasps.

Joseph's outburst was more than Martha could resist and in spite of her embarrassment, she too erupted into unrestrained laughter.

Pursing his lips and taking in a deep breath, the ruddy-faced man's head began to shake. He reached beneath his seat and brought out a pillow. Without saying a word, he covered his face and put his head back against the wall.

"We're terrible, Joseph. You know that don't you?" Martha stood up and made her way to the restroom at the back of the plane.

Joseph had regained his composure by the time Martha returned to her seat. The man by the window appeared to be sleeping again.

"We really must apologize to him," Martha said to Joseph.

"You're right, we should. But don't you think he looked like a circus clown?" Joseph asked rhetorically. "Anyway, we'll clear things up when we land."

"Don't be surprised if he refuses to speak to us," Martha warned. "Not that I'd blame him."

"Well, I didn't mean any harm. Besides, he seems to be sleeping again." Joseph put his seat in a reclined position as he continued. "Now tell me more about you and Paul. How did you get together after the incident at the cabin?"

"I'll only tell you if you promise not to make me laugh anymore," Martha said.

Joseph smiled and nodded in agreement.

"When I saw that I had hit him with the rock, I got scared and ran," Martha said. "My friends picked up our things and followed right behind me. After a short distance it was obvious that we weren't being followed. Paul admitted later that he was too shocked to even think of chasing us."

"So how did you actually meet?" Joseph asked.

"It was at a dance the next evening. I was standing near the punch bowl when he came over for a glass of punch. I wasn't sure how to react when I saw the bump on his head and realized that he recognized me, but he was very gracious." Martha's eyes sparkled as she spoke.

"What did he say?" Joseph quizzed.

"He asked me to dance," Martha replied. "In fact, he never mentioned our first meeting."

"I don't think I would have dared either," Joseph suggested.

"No, it wasn't like that," Martha returned. "There was something there that night at the dance. It was like an immediate connection between us. More than just an attraction, it was some kind of a feeling."

Captivated by Martha's account of that evening, Joseph was able to do little more than nod appropriately as she spoke.

"Paul was always the perfect gentleman and oh could he dance." Martha's head began to gently sway back-and-forth as if she could hear the music from that night. "We danced that evening until our feet were sore. When the band finished playing, Paul hummed some tunes so we could keep dancing. They had to practically kick us out of the auditorium."

Martha drew in a deep breath and sighed before continuing. "Paul asked if he could take me for an ice cream soda before I went home, but it was late and as much as I hated to, I declined his invitation. 'Well,' he said as we parted, 'there's always tomorrow.' Somehow I knew I'd see him again."

"Please go on," Joseph requested after several seconds of silence.

"I didn't give him my telephone number or anything, but Paul managed to find me. We went dancing every Friday until summer break. Then the war interfered. Paul was drafted and sent to Korea." The sparkle in Martha's eyes turned to a glisten, and a tear rolled down each cheek. "I'll never forget when he shipped out. We held each other until he had to board the train. He ran to the nearest open window and reached out for me. We held hands as long as we could. As the train pulled away from the platform, my hand slipped from his and I wondered what had happened to my world. 'Just remember,' Paul yelled from the open window, 'there's always tomorrow.' And there always was."

Joseph noticed that Martha was crying. "I can't imagine sending a loved one off to war," he said as he took the napkin from her tray-table and placed it in her hand.

"I knew I'd see him again," Martha said as she wiped her eyes. "We were very fortunate. The war ended about a year after Paul was drafted and he remained in the Service for about three months after the armistice. We were apart for less than two years."

"I guess it could have been worse, but still . . ."

Martha interrupted Joseph's comment. "A lot of people had it worse than we did. Some of our friends went off to war never to return and I knew in my heart that Paul would be back. Don't get me wrong, there were times when I was scared. But it always kept me going."

"What kept you going?" Joseph asked.

"Paul's optimism. He always looked at the bright side of things. He ended every letter with 'There's always tomorrow.' It seemed to be his theme in life and it became our family motto. The kids didn't always understand, but it made sense as they got older. At least to most of them." Martha's voice trailed off as she turned her head and stared up the aisle.

"How soon were you married after Paul got home?" Joseph queried.

"He got home in October, and we were married in December. The rest, as they say, is history." Martha turned and looked at Joseph. "Have I bored you enough?" she asked.

"You haven't bored me at all. In fact I'd like to hear more. Tell me about your children."

Martha reached into her handbag and pulled out a wallet-sized photo album. She opened it to reveal several photographs in plastic holders. "This is James," she said pointing to the first picture. "He's my oldest. He took after his father and works as an engineer. Here he is with his wife and three children," she said as she pulled a photo from behind the first one. She pointed to another portrait. "This is Mary with her husband and two children. And here is Rachel and her twin sister

Anna. Rachel's married now, but I still don't have a picture of her with her husband. They don't have any children yet."

"They look . . . hmm . . ." Joseph said pointing at the photo of the twins.

"Anna is still single," Martha interrupted as she winked at Joseph.

Joseph blushed. "And who's this?" he said pointing at the last picture as if he hadn't heard Martha's footnote.

"This is Thomas. He's my youngest and he's not married either," Martha responded.

"You must be very proud of your children," Joseph said.

"And my grandchildren," Martha added.

"Won't they miss you over the holidays?" Joseph asked.

"No," Martha replied, "I'll be home on Christmas Eve, just in time for our family dinner."

"Then your children live near you," Joseph surmised.

"The four oldest live within a few minutes of my home. I see them at least two or three times a week."

"And your youngest, Thomas is it?" Joseph asked.

Martha didn't respond and acted as though she didn't intend to. Joseph thought it best to change the subject.

"How about a picture of Paul? I didn't see one of him in your collection," Joseph observed.

"I don't have a picture of him that will fit in here," Martha responded. "It would be nice to have a picture so others could see him, but I don't really need one because

I can always picture him in my mind. You'll just have to trust me when I tell you he was one of the most handsome men a woman ever set her eyes on."

Martha's thoughts were interrupted by the flight attendant.

"May I take those for you?" the hostess asked as she gestured towards the trash remaining from their snack.

Martha cleared both hers and Joseph's tray. "Thank you," she said as she handed the cups and napkins to the young woman. "I think I'll keep these for later," Martha said and placed the bag of pretzels in her purse.

"We'll be landing soon, so you'll need to put your seats upright and make sure your seat belts are fastened," the flight attendant said as she moved to the next row of seats.

Martha smiled and nodded.

"Thanks," Joseph added as he brought the back of his seat forward.

The captain's deep voice sounded over the intercom announcing the beginning of their descent into Atlanta.

"I sure appreciate your willingness to visit with me," Martha said to Joseph.

"I should be the one thanking you Martha. This is without a doubt the most enjoyable flight I have ever had."

"In spite of the fact that I did all the talking?" Martha asked. She gently laid her open hand on Joseph's leg. "I don't know a thing about you."

"Well, there isn't much to know," Joseph responded. "I live alone in Atlanta and work in sales. My only hobby is reading and I don't have any interesting stories to share with people I meet on airplanes."

"I'm not sure I believe that," Martha returned emphatically, "but I don't know if I could have survived this flight without you. Your listening ear helped keep my nerves at bay."

"Don't mention it. I'm a good listener."

As the plane landed and taxied to the gate, Martha took her compact from her purse and made some necessary adjustments to her appearance. Joseph took the newspaper he had never finished reading and put it in his briefcase.

The man seated by the window moved the pillow from off his face and looked around with obvious determination not to make eye contact with Joseph or Martha. He took a comb from his breast pocket and smoothed down his hair.

"I hope you'll forgive our little outburst," Joseph said to the man.

"Excuse me," was his expressionless reply as he stood and made his way to the aisle. He opened the overhead bin, took out a bag and moved to the forward door.

"He could have at least nodded," Martha said in horror.

"It's okay, Martha. We tried," Joseph chuckled. "Anyway, you were the one who said you wouldn't blame him if he didn't speak to us."

"I know," she admitted, "but the seatbelt sign is still on."

Joseph smiled and shook his head.

Martha waited to stand until the seatbelt indicator light turned off. She moved into the aisle and pressed toward the door with the rest of the passengers. Joseph pulled his bag from overhead and followed closely behind.

Martha moved with the crowd into the airport concourse. Her anxiety level began to increase as she looked around. As far as she could see in both directions, there were people.

"Let's see where you catch your connecting flight," Joseph said above the quiet roar as he ushered Martha to a monitor displaying departure information.

Martha handed Joseph her ticket.

"Your plane leaves from Concourse D," Joseph said. "Right now we're in Concourse A."

Martha nodded in understanding.

Joseph continued. "I'm going to the terminal, so we can go as far as the people movers together."

"What are people movers?" Martha asked.

"They're like train cars that will take us where we need to go," Joseph answered.

He took Martha by the arm and walked with her down the long corridor to some stairs. They descended the stairs to what looked like the deck at a train station. Shiny silver cars pulled up to the platform and dozens of people forced their way on while a like number squeezed through onto the platform. Then the cars sped away.

"See how the different areas are marked with colors?" Joseph asked. "Each color represents a different destination."

"What color do I want?" Martha queried.

"Green. Concourse D is green," Joseph replied.

Joseph walked with Martha to the designated area of the platform.

"The next set of cars that stop here will take you to your concourse," Joseph said.

"And what do I do when I get there?"

"Then you take the stairs back up to the main corridor and find Gate 7. That's where you'll board your plane," Joseph replied.

"I can do that," Martha responded confidently.

"This is where I have to leave you," Joseph said as he extended his right hand toward Martha.

Martha stretched out her arms and wrapped them around Joseph's large chest. "Thanks again," she said.

"You take care of yourself and enjoy that cruise," Joseph said as he gently took Martha by the wrists and slid her hands into his. "And thanks for sharing part of your life with me."

"You're welcome," Martha responded. "You have a Merry Christmas, Joseph"

Joseph reached into his shirt pocket and pulled out a business card. "You too, Martha. And keep in touch," he added as he placed the card into Martha's hand and walked away.

Martha waved as Joseph disappeared into the crowd.

CHAPTER THREE

The silver rail car pulled rapidly to the platform in front of Martha and made an abrupt stop.

"I can do this," Martha muttered under her breath.

She was shocked when the crowd of people making their way onto the newly arrived people mover pushed her from behind. Like a grain of sand being pushed through a sieve, she was forced forward through the throng of people trying to exit the same car. Once inside, she was sandwiched between people of all shapes and sizes. Suddenly the car surged forward with a jerk causing Martha to lose her footing.

"Whoa little lady!"

Martha found herself in the arms of the man standing next to her. The wide brimmed Stetson hat seated firmly on his head enhanced his large stature. A well-trimmed beard, cowboy boots, and western-cut corduroy jacket with leather elbow patches were consistent with Martha's image of a Southern Gentleman.

"Let's see if we can keep y'all upright while here in Atlanta," he drawled.

The broad Southern accent completed the picture in Martha's mind.

"Just hang on right here and you'll stay in the saddle," he said as he took her hand and placed it on a strap hanging from the roof of the car.

Martha noticed a small sprig of plastic mistletoe tucked into her rescuer's hatband.

"Thank you," she responded nervously.

"Don't mention it," he returned as he tipped his hat, and resumed his conversation with the man at his left.

In spite of his kindness, Martha was relieved that the man didn't expect her to reward him in the traditional Holiday fashion.

The crowded car sped through its underground tunnel at such speed that the view from the windows was nothing more than a blur. Martha was beginning to feel dizzy and uncomfortable when the car slowed slightly. With a jolt, it stopped as suddenly as it had taken off. Her firm grip on the plastic strap prevented a repeat of her earlier stumble.

The same forces that moved Martha into the car now conveyed her onto the platform below Concourse D. She moved to the stairs and ascended to a corridor that looked almost identical to the one she had left only minutes earlier.

Martha stood at the top of the stairs and gazed around until she felt oriented to her surroundings. Still rattled from her short but harrowing ride through the bowels of the airport, she was anxious to find a place to sit and recover. Locating the signs pointing her in the appropriate direction, Martha began moving toward Gate 7.

"You can do this Martha," she kept repeating to herself as she made her way through the crowd. Occasional glimpses of festive decorations and advertisements helped to brighten her dampened spirit.

She was glad to find an empty chair where she could relax for a few minutes before boarding the plane. As she sat, Martha stared at the jet parked outside the gate. It was obviously larger than the one she had arrived on. She reached into her handbag, took out her ticket and examined the boarding pass. "Seat 34A," she said aloud. She was excited about the prospects of a window seat on this flight.

Martha placed the ticket back into her large purse, then searched through the rest of its contents until she found the pretzels she had placed there earlier. She opened the bag and began to snack. She wasn't particularly hungry, but this was a good way to pass the time.

"Is anyone sitting here?"

Martha looked up to see a young man pointing to the seat next to hers. "I don't think so," she said. "I'm sure someone just left that newspaper there."

The young man picked up the newspaper and placed it on the floor beneath the seat. "If you don't mind, I think I'll join you," he said as he sat down, obviously not seeking Martha's permission. He was casually dressed in cut-off blue jeans, a T-shirt, and a pair of leather sandals. Perched on top of his head was a red Santa Claus hat. A pair of dark glasses clung to the hat just above the white fur cuff.

Realizing that she was still wearing her coat, Martha wondered why the young man wasn't cold in his summer attire. She smiled but said nothing.

"You off to Puerto Rico too?" he asked.

"Yes I am," Martha responded.

"For Christmas?" he asked. "No," he proceeded

without giving Martha time to reply, "you're probably headed for one of those cruises, huh?"

"That's right," she acknowledged.

"Not me!" he said. "I'm going to paaarty."

"That's..."

The young man continued as though he hadn't even heard Martha's attempted response. "I go there every few months and stay until I have just enough money to get back home. I come home, find a job and as soon as I've earned enough money, it's back to the fun."

Martha nodded periodically as he continued describing his activities on the beaches of San Juan. When the call came to begin boarding the plane, she was truly ready.

"I've got to go now," Martha said, interrupting his monologue for a speedy escape. "They're calling for my row."

As she stood up and moved into the line of passengers waiting to board the plane, something fell to the floor from her lap.

"Hey lady, you dropped this," the young man called after her. He ran to Martha's side and handed her the piece of paper.

"Thank you," she said taking the paper from his hand.

"Yeah, okay. Have a good cruise," he said and took his place at the end of the line.

Though it seemed busier, Martha felt less anxious than when she boarded the plane bound for Atlanta. The atmosphere was notably different. The larger interior seemed to make it brighter, but quieter. Due to the increased length of the flight, there was more preparatory activity among the flight attendants. As she moved further towards the back of the plane and her seat, Martha could hear the clanging of utensils in the galley.

After getting settled in her seat, Martha realized she was still clutching the paper the young man had picked up and returned to her. She opened her hand to reveal the business card Joseph had given her as he left. It must have fallen out of my purse when I took out the pretzels, she thought. She read what was printed on the card: Joseph Watkins, Sales Representative, Parkinson Distributing, Atlanta, Georgia. "I wonder what he sells?" she said to herself as she placed the card back into her purse.

Martha sat quietly and watched her fellow passengers board the plane. Patiently she waited to see who would be sitting next to her. A small, very pretty young woman with dark eyes and matching complexion soon seated herself next to Martha.

"Hello," Martha said.

The woman smiled and nodded.

"You don't speak English do you?" Martha asked with no expectation of receiving an answer.

"No Ingles," the women replied in what Martha assumed to be a Puerto Rican accent.

Now it was Martha's turn to smile and nod.

Looking around and listening to the conversations of other passengers, it became painfully obvious that very few people seated around her actually spoke English. She was somewhat disappointed at not having anyone to visit with during the flight, but she was a little tired and decided this would allow her to nap without appearing to be rude.

When everyone was seated, the plane began to move and the flight attendants began their safety presentation. Martha listened intently once again. She knew that they would be flying over water this time and wanted to be prepared in the event of an emergency. Her confidence was boosted by the fact that she remembered most of the instructions from the flight to Atlanta.

As the nose of the plane lifted, Martha thought of Joseph and what he had said about take-off and landing being the best parts of the flight. She was inclined to agree with him.

Taking her itinerary from her purse, Martha opened to the page outlining her schedule in Puerto Rico. Arriving in San Juan at 7:00 p.m. local time, she would have an hour to get her luggage and catch the shuttle to her ship, which would set sail at 10:00 p.m. Her travel agent assured her she would have sufficient time.

Martha jerked when her head slumped forward, her chin hitting her chest. "I must be more tired than I thought," she said to herself. She placed the itinerary back into her purse, reclined her seat and allowed sleep to overtake her.

"Ma'am."

Someone placed their hand on Martha's shoulder and shook her gently.

"Ma'am," the voice repeated. "We'll be landing soon. You need to put your seat in the upright position." The flight attendant smiled at Martha as she opened her eyes.

Martha took in a deep breath and let it out slowly. "Thank you," she said and brought the back of her seat forward.

The captain announced the beginning of their descent into San Juan. As the plane banked, Martha looked out at the sites below. There were rows and rows of buildings that appeared to be nothing more than boxes: one and two story cement boxes. Wooden power poles hoisted wires that seemed to be running every-where like a giant spider-web over the structures. Large clusters of green plants and palm trees were scattered throughout. The city was surrounded by water except for distant mountains and lush green rolling hills in the foreground. Taller buildings became visible as they neared the end of the runway and touchdown.

The exhilaration of landing made Martha think of Joseph once again.

Martha peered out the window as the plane taxied from the runway and came to a complete stop at the airport gate. She waited in her seat until there was a sufficient break in the flow of passengers to move into the aisle and file out of the plane with everyone else.

As she stepped from the plane's interior, Martha suddenly felt as if she was being forced to breath through a wet blanket. "This sure is different from the weather at home this time of year," she mumbled, "and I hope I can get used to this humidity,"

Inside the airport, the air conditioning gave some relief from the heaviness of the warm moist air, but didn't seem to help her anxiety. Martha removed her coat and put it over her arm. Now she stood a little confused as she looked around. "Relax Martha," she said to herself. "Now think." She surveyed her surroundings and located a sign depicting a suitcase. Assuming it would lead to the baggage claim area, she moved in the direction it pointed. After a short distance she found signs printed in both Spanish and English that led to her intended destination at the end of the corridor.

Martha could feel herself becoming more uneasy as she waited for luggage to begin arriving at the claim area. Across the carousel, she spotted a Santa Claus hat. She watched in anticipation as the young man from the airport in Atlanta moved in her direction. Instinctively, she moved to be near him.

"Hey," he said as Martha walked toward him. "I see you made it."

"Yes," Martha responded, "I made it."

"The bags will start coming soon. How many do you have?"

"Just two," she replied.

"Two?" the young man asked. "How long you plannin' on stayin'— a month?"

"Only a week," Martha said with a chuckle.

"I can live a couple of months easy on just the stuff in my one backpack." He continued, "Oh well, I guess that's a woman for you. Have to pack everything just in case."

"I suppose you're right." Martha continued without taking a breath in order to avoid being cut off mid-sentence. "Listen, I wanted to thank you for returning that card to me and I'd like to know your name."

Martha was surprised by her sudden willingness to talk to this young man. But in this strange place, he seemed like an old friend.

"Jim. And you already thanked me," he replied.

"Jim, huh? I assume that's short for James?" Martha said.

"Yep, but don't call me that. Only my mother and my preacher call me that and that's just 'cause I don't dare tell them I don't like it."

"I'm glad you have that kind of respect for your mother James, I mean Jim," Martha said. "My oldest son is named James."

"Does he go by Jim?"

"No, he's James to everyone," she said.

Before he could respond, the conveyor began to move and Jim spotted his pack. As it moved in front of him, he lifted it from the carousel and placed it over one shoulder.

"Do you want me to help you with your bags before I go?" Jim asked.

"No, they're not that heavy. But thank you for offering," Martha replied.

"Okay. Well, I'm going to grab me something to eat and catch a guagua to the beach."

The mention of food made Martha realize that she was hungry. She had slept through the meal on the plane.

"Where can I get something to eat in a hurry?" Martha queried.

"There are vendors in the main terminal near the front of the airport. But don't eat the pinchos. They look like lamb kabobs, but I hear they're made of dog meat. Stick to what you know."

"Thank you James, I mean Jim." Martha said.

"It's okay, you can call me James. Maybe I'll see you 'round sometime. Enjoy your cruise," Jim said as he walked away.

Martha turned back to the baggage conveyer. She was relieved to see her bags and soon had them by her side. Moving to a nearby bench, Martha opened one of her bags and placed her coat inside. "I won't be needing this here," she said aloud.

With the strap of one bag over her shoulder and the other one in hand, Martha set out to find the shuttle pick-up point. By following others who had retrieved their luggage, she easily found her way to the main terminal.

Though she was in a foreign country, Martha could see the obvious American influence in the airport. There were newsstands, food vendors, gift shops and even followers of Krishna spreading their message to anyone who would listen. But there were differences as well. There didn't seem to be anything in the way of holiday decorations, the smell was somehow unusual and the manner of dress was not quite what she was used to. Not that there was anything wrong with these differences, but somehow everything just seemed so—casual.

The cruise company shuttle was near the main entrance of the airport. Martha made her way to the curb and checked her bags with the driver who loaded them on the small bus. She had 20 minutes before the shuttle left, so Martha set out to find something to eat.

Back inside, she found a cart where several different food items were offered. Though the pinchos looked good, Martha took Jim's advice and steered away from them. Nothing was particularly appealing, but the hotdogs seemed the safest.

The last time Martha could remember eating a hotdog purchased from a vendor was at the state high school basketball finals. She and Paul had gone to watch Thomas play in the final game of his senior year. They ate hotdogs at half time. As usual, Paul buried his in onions and Martha smothered hers with mustard.

After taking her hotdog and loading it with mustard, Martha found a bench where she could sit and enjoy her meal. Except for the bag of pretzels in Atlanta, she hadn't eaten since breakfast. The smell of the spicy mustard covering the meat made her mouth water even before she started eating. Every bite was as satisfying as she expected.

Martha finished eating and got up to return to the shuttle. "Drats!" she exclaimed as she noticed a large blotch of mustard on the front of her white blouse. "That will never come out."

She found a restroom and hurried in to attack the stain. She wiped off what she could with a paper towel, but that seemed to only smear it. Taking her handkerchief from her purse, she wet it and then wet the spot on the blouse. She added soap from the dispenser on the wall and began scrubbing with her fingers.

While Martha stood at the sink furiously rubbing the ugly smear, another woman in the restroom approached. "You need help?" the woman asked in broken-English.

Seeing the multiple stains on the woman's T-shirt, Martha wondered if she should be offering to help her. The woman had a slight build and was probably about Martha's age. Her dark curly hair was graying and looked as though it hadn't seen a brush in several days.

"Thank you, no," Martha replied. "I think I'm getting it.

"I be here if you need." The woman smiled and proceeded to wash her grimy hands in a neighboring basin.

Gradually, the spot changed from deep ocher to pale yellow. "Well, at least it's less noticeable," Martha said out loud as she dried it the best she could with a clean paper towel.

She smiled at the woman next to her as she left the restroom and returned to the terminal and the shuttle pick-up. As she walked through the door and over to the curb, Martha felt the pit of her stomach tighten and a sudden sense of fear gripped her heart. The shuttle bus was gone. She looked at her watch. It was 8:10 p.m.

CHAPTER FOUR

"Oh, now what do I do? I'm going to miss the ship. They have my luggage and everything. What do I do, what do I do?" Martha began to cry.

After a moment, she composed herself. She took a deep breath and wiped her eyes. "Now take it easy. Crying isn't going to help anything. Think Martha, think," she repeated to herself.

Martha walked back inside the airport. She found a bench along a wall and slumped into it. "All right," she said after taking a deep breath, "there's no time to waste."

She sat quietly for a moment while collecting her thoughts. The cruise company must come here a lot. Certainly there is someone here that can help me. There's got to be an Information desk or something like that.

Martha assessed her surroundings. Along the back wall directly in front of the main entrance to the airport she spotted what looked like it could be an information desk. She stood and walked across the lobby toward the area until the sign posted above the counter became visible: Information. "Oh, thank goodness," she said.

"Excuse me! Miss, can you help me?" Martha inquired of the attendant seated behind the counter.

The olive skinned woman had large brown eyes and

a warm smile. "What can I do for you?" she asked in accented, but clear English.

"I'm so glad you speak English," Martha said.

Martha's obvious relief made the young woman's smile increase in size.

Martha continued. "Yes, I need you to help me get in touch with these people." She handed the woman a brochure that came with her itinerary.

"Is there a problem?" she inquired.

"Yes. You see I hadn't eaten all day, so after leaving my luggage at the shuttle I went and bought something to eat." Martha's tension was obvious as her speech became progressively more rapid and she began gesturing with her hands. "I was eating a hotdog and spilled mustard on my blouse. I went into the restroom to clean it off and while I was in there, the shuttle left without me. I need them to come back and get me so I don't miss my cruise."

The young woman tilted her head slightly as she listened to Martha. Her confused expression made Martha wonder if she could understand English as well as she spoke it.

"Listen," Martha continued anxiously, "can you just call and see if they have another shuttle or can send that one back for me?"

The woman nodded. "Okay, I'll call them," she said.

Walking back to the desk behind the counter, the young lady picked up the telephone and dialed the number listed on the brochure. She began speaking Spanish into the receiver.

Martha became increasingly nervous as she waited

for the conversation to conclude. Looking at her watch, she noted that it was now 8:25 p.m. After several minutes, the woman returned.

"I spoke to someone with the cruise company. They said the shuttle that just left from here is the only one available at the moment and it hasn't arrived there yet. They expect it soon, but once it arrives, they still need to unload it. They're afraid that won't leave enough time to come back for you and return to the port before it's time to board the ship."

"So what am I supposed to do?" Martha asked. It was all she could do to keep from crying.

"They suggest you take a taxi to the pier. You should still be able to get there in time if you hurry," she said reassuringly. "They'll be looking for you, but said if you're not there by 9:30, they can't let you board."

"Thank you," Martha said as she turned and walked toward the front of the airport. She still had many questions, but knew there was no time to ask them.

Martha had never ridden in a taxi and wasn't too excited about the prospects of her first experience being in a foreign country. As she stepped outside, all she could think about was Sarah's comment earlier that morning. A woman should never ride alone in a taxi. The words kept playing over and over in her mind like a recorded message. A woman should never ride alone in a taxi.

She hadn't noticed all the activity outside when she left her luggage at the shuttle, but this time, her focus had changed. As she peered down the sidewalk, Martha could see a steady stream of yellow taxis dropping-off and picking-up passengers at the curbside. Each one, in turn, would come to a sudden halt, causing the back of the vehicle to rise up momentarily. In like fashion, all of them darted out into traffic with a blaring horn as the only indication of their intentions. She couldn't see any of the passengers, but imagined their faces with expressions of sheer terror.

"I don't want to do this," she said. "But what else can I do? Maybe there's a bus that can take me there."

Intending to ask the girl at the Information Desk if there was another alternative to a taxi, Martha went back inside. As she passed through the door, she came face-to-face with the woman from the restroom. This is odd, Martha thought. It was almost as if the woman had been waiting for her.

"You need help now?" the woman asked in the same broken-English. "I get you to boat."

"How?" Martha asked. "Is there a bus?"

"Guagua," the woman answered.

Martha had no idea what guagua meant. "I'm sorry, I don't understand gwa-gwa," she said.

"Guagua take you to boat. I take you to guagua, guagua take you to boat," the woman explained insistently.

The whole idea of going with this woman made Martha feel uneasy, but the thought of riding in a taxi was more troubling.

"Guagua!" Martha said. "Oh yes, James said he was taking a guagau to the beach. All right, you take me to the guagua."

"You come. Hurry," the woman said as she escorted

Martha back outside. Taking Martha by the hand, she began running and pulling Martha behind. They dodged traffic as they crossed the busy street. Soon a large passenger van, similar to those Martha was familiar with at home, pulled up to the curb.

"Guagua," the woman said pointing at the van. She opened the side door and helped Martha step inside.

Although it was designed to accommodate 12 passengers, the van looked as if it was already crammed beyond capacity. One woman had a child on her lap. One young man was kneeling on the floor and another was standing hunched-over so his head didn't hit the roof.

"Sit," the woman said to Martha. She pointed to a small space between a rather large man and the armrest of the seat closest to the door.

Martha squeezed into the space. The woman pulled the door shut, said something in Spanish to the driver and knelt down next to Martha.

I can't believe I'm doing this, Martha thought. She leaned over to the woman. "I need to be at the pier before 9:30. Will we make it?"

"Sí," the woman responded. "We make it."

The man sitting to the left of Martha was emitting a most unpleasant odor. The smell was somewhere between cigarette smoke and dirty laundry, or perhaps both. He was wearing a filthy T-shirt with Hogar Crea imprinted on the front. Martha leaned closer to the open window in the door so she could take-in some of the fresh air from outside.

Martha watched out the window as the van drove

away from the airport. She wasn't sure whether to be intrigued or frightened by her circumstances. "Just remember, there's always tomorrow," she thought. "I'm sure I'll be able to look back and laugh."

It only took a short distance for Martha to decide that the guagua driver must have received the same training as the taxi drivers. Every stop was sudden and every turn without warning. It appeared that his hand never left the horn button.

Every driver of every vehicle seemed aggressive. Martha wondered why they bothered with stoplights as few people paid any attention to them. Pedestrians were everywhere, including the middle of the intersections.

People could be seen selling small bananas and cookies. Some of them were wearing T-shirts bearing the same Hogar Crea imprint as her neighbor's. Over the noise of the traffic she could hear what sounded like "cheeklay" being yelled by the young children peddling gum.

Martha wondered why she did not see any Christmas decorations on the businesses or lampposts. Perhaps it was because of the warm weather, but even the houses were devoid of the traditional seasonal trimmings she was used to at home.

"How much longer?" Martha asked her self-appointed guide.

"How you say? Uh . . . ten minute," she responded.

"I hope I can survive another ten minutes," Martha muttered.

The further they got from the airport, the more the scenery changed. The roads went from concrete to cobblestone and became much narrower. At some places, there was barely room for two vehicles to pass each other without driving onto the narrow sidewalks. Buildings went from being somewhat modern looking to older stucco type structures.

The landscape was not the only thing that was changing. Martha was becoming increasingly uneasy with each mile they traveled. The sun was going down, leaving streetlamps as the major source of light. The shadow filled streets only added to Martha's growing fear. It was now 9:05 p.m. and more than ten minutes since she had last inquired about their timetable.

The woman stood up and yelled something to the driver. The van came to a sudden stop. The driver got out of the van and came around to the side. Opening the door, he helped the woman and Martha onto the side-walk.

"You pay," the woman said to Martha.

"Oh, of course," Martha said. She opened her handbag and took out some money. "This is the smallest I have," she said holding up a ten-dollar bill. "Do you have change?"

The young driver smiled as he snatched the money from Martha's hand. He placed it in his shirt pocket, returned to the van and started the motor.

"Hey!" Martha yelled after him as he drove away. She looked at the woman. "Did you know he'd do that?"

The woman's only response was a feigned look of innocence.

The street where they were standing was quiet and poorly illuminated. In the distance, Martha could see the flicker of lights and the shadowy outline of a ship. "Is that where we're going?" she asked the woman.

"Sí. Yes," she responded. "We be there soon. We go this way."

"Couldn't we have driven all the way there?" Martha inquired.

"Come," the woman responded as she started crossing the street.

Martha hesitated.

"Come quickly!" the woman insisted, motioning for Martha to follow.

Something told her that things weren't right. In spite of her apprehension, Martha knew she was at the woman's mercy. She had no choice but to follow.

On the other side of the street, the woman walked along the sidewalk for about a block, then turned down an alley. Martha walked several paces behind. As she entered the alley, she could not see the woman.

"Where are you?" she called.

"Come, we must hurry," the woman called from the darkness.

Cautiously, Martha entered the alley and began walking into the shadows.

"Hurry," the woman called again.

"I'm coming," Martha said, too quietly to be heard.

Martha's steps had slowed to the point that she was barely moving. She gasped when someone grabbed her arm from somewhere in the darkness.

"Oh," she sighed in relief. "It's only you."

The woman had a firm grip on Martha's bicep. "Give me purse!" the woman ordered.

"What?" Martha asked. "What are you doing?"

The woman shook Martha's arm. "Give me purse," she repeated more emphatically.

Martha stood in silent disbelief, too scared to move.

The woman threw Martha to the ground. She pulled a gun from under her shirt and pointed it at Martha.

"No, please!" Martha pleaded. "Not that. Please don't hurt me."

A terror-filled scream pierced the still night air.

CHAPTER FIVE

"Mr. Cooper, your wife is on the line."

"Thanks Jenni," James called to his secretary.

"Hi Honey, what's up?"

"James, I got an interesting telephone call a few minutes ago," Elizabeth said. Her voice was quiet and James had to strain in order to hear.

"Who was it?" James asked.

"Chief Rosen from the Police Department," Elizabeth replied.

"Chief Rosen? What did he want?"

"He asked for you. He said you need to call him right away."

"That's all he said? I need to call him?" James' mind began to race as he tried to come up with a reason that the Chief of Police would want to speak with him. "Why didn't you just have him call me here?"

"I offered to give him your number," Elizabeth responded, "but he said he didn't want to interrupt you, but to have you call him as soon as you have a few minutes to talk."

"That's it?" James asked.

"Nothing else, except not to worry," Elizabeth said. "But James, he sounded worried."

"All right. I guess I'll call and see what he wants. I'll call you back after I talk to him. Love you."

James sat with the receiver in his hand for several

seconds before hanging up.

"Why would he want to talk to me?" he said out loud as he took the telephone directory from the top drawer of his desk. His hand was shaking as he found the page and ran his finger down the column to the correct number.

James carefully dialed the number. With each ring came another thought about the reason for the call.

"Police Department."

"Hello. Yes, this is James Cooper. I have a message to call Chief Rosen."

"One moment Mr. Cooper. I'll transfer you now."

"Thank you," James said. His mind continued to race as he listened to the Christmas music playing while he waited.

"This is Chief Rosen."

"Chief, this is James Cooper. My wife said you called." James' mouth became dry and he could feel his heart beating in his throat.

"Thank you for calling back Mr. Cooper, I'll get right to the point," the Chief said. "Do you know Martha Cooper?"

"Yes, she's my mother, but she's on a Caribbean cruise and won't be home until Sunday," James replied.

"Well Mr. Cooper, I received a telephone call from the Police in San Juan, Puerto Rico early this morning." Chief Rosen paused.

James could feel his chest getting heavy. "Is Mom okay?" he asked.

"I'm afraid not, Mr. Cooper. She was found dead in San Juan last night."

"That's not possible," James argued. "The cruise left

from San Juan on Sunday. How could they find her there on Tuesday?"

"According to the San Juan Police, she was found in the back of an alley in an area called Old San Juan. Not a very safe area from what they tell me."

James sat in silence as the chief continued, "They're not sure what she was doing there, but apparently she was the victim of a robbery. They think she may have been lured away from the airport and then taken to the city and robbed. Her purse was with her, but there wasn't much in it. No money or credit cards anyway."

Silence continued on James' end of the telephone.

"Are you still there Mr. Cooper?" the chief asked.

"Yes, I'm still here," James said. "I just don't know what to say."

"I understand," Chief Rosen acknowledged before continuing. "The details are quite sketchy, but if you have any questions, I'll do my best to answer them."

James had so many questions that he didn't know where to begin. "So how did they know to contact you?"

"There was an ID card in your mother's purse with her name, address and all the usual information. They faxed me a copy of it. That's where I got your name and number," the chief responded.

"How did she actually die?" James hesitantly inquired. He wasn't sure he wanted to hear the answer, but knew he would always wonder if he didn't ask.

"There was a gunshot wound to her chest. She prob-ably went quickly," the chief replied.

"I guess that's better than being beaten and left to die," James said. Tears began to run down his cheeks as he continued with his questions. "So now what?"

"I wish I could give you a definite answer, but I'm afraid we're not quite sure. We do know that the San Juan Police want to keep the body there until they finish their investigation. That will include an autopsy."

"Is there a need for that?" James asked.

"I think it's appropriate," Chief Rosen answered. "They'll want to confirm that the gunshot wound was the cause of death. Anyway, that means the investigation will take a little longer. I gather from my conversation with them that they do things a little differently than we do here, so I'm not sure how long everything will take."

"Any guesses?" James asked.

"The autopsy will only take a day. The problem is, they said it will be at least two days before they get to it," the chief explained.

"So she could be back here by the weekend?"

"I don't think I would count on that. If the autopsy is completed Friday, there are some legal things that need to be done before the body can be released for return to the U.S. Since Puerto Rico is a U.S. Territory, that part should be as easy as working with another state, but the weekend could complicate things a little and then with Monday being Christmas, who knows?"

"Then what do you think is a reasonable expectation?" James asked.

"I think Tuesday is the most likely," he said.

"I see," James sighed. "So she won't be home for Christmas."

"I'm afraid I wouldn't count on it, Mr. Cooper," the chief replied.

"Is there anything else you need from me right now?" James asked.

"No, I think we'll just have to wait to hear from the police down there. As soon as they contact me, I'll get in touch with you and we can finish making the necessary arrangements."

"I'll wait to hear from you then. Good-bye and thank you," James said.

"Good-bye Mr. Cooper and I'm sorry about your loss," Chief Rosen said and hung up the phone.

"This isn't the way it was supposed to be Mom," James said out loud. He began to reflect on the last time that he saw his mother alive. His secretary interrupted his thoughts.

"Mr. Cooper, your 11:00 appointment just called and said they . . . are you okay?" she asked after seeing his tear-filled eyes.

"I'll be fine. You were saying about my appointment?"

"They need to reschedule," Jenni replied.

"That's fine Jenni. I need to go home. Can you cancel the rest of today's appointments?"

"Sure," she said. "What should I tell them?"

"Tell them my mother just died and I'll contact them next week," he said. James closed his brief case, took his overcoat from the coat tree and headed for the door.

"Mr. Cooper..." Jenni stopped as though she didn't know what to say next. "Mr. Cooper, is there anything I can do for you?"

"Thank you Jenni. I'll be fine. I'll talk to you tomorrow."

As James left the office and walked to his car, he thought about how he was going to break the news to the rest of his family. Being the oldest, it seemed that it was expected of him to take charge in times of crisis. Difficult tasks had been his in the past. He recalled the day he was sent to find Thomas at school and inform him that their father had just died.

The ten-minute drive home seemed to take hours, yet James remembered little about it. Elizabeth was doing dishes at the kitchen sink when he entered through the back door.

"What are you doing home?" Elizabeth asked. She dried her hands and continued before giving James time to answer. "It's about the call from the police, isn't it?"

"We need to talk." James replied. He took Elizabeth by the hand and led her into the front room. Seating her on the sofa, he pulled the rocking chair so it was facing her and sat down.

"What is it James?"

James inhaled deeply then exhaled slowly. "It's about Mom."

"What about her?" Elizabeth asked. "Sarah said she got to the airport and I haven't heard of any plane crashes or sinking boats."

"Apparently she was robbed in San Juan. They're not sure of the circumstances, but her body was found in an alley in the city." James' chin and lower lip began to quiver. "She had been shot in the chest."

Elizabeth's eyes welled with tears as she leaned

forward in her seat and fell into James' arms. "Why?" she sobbed. "Why her? Why now?"

Elizabeth's mother had died shortly after she and James were married. Martha had truly accepted Elizabeth as one of her own children. Though she was never one to interfere, Martha was always there to offer support or a shoulder to cry on. She and James both knew that if there were ever problems in his marriage, Martha would be likely to come to Elizabeth's defense.

James held Elizabeth tightly and caressed her back with his open hand. After several minutes, he lifted her chin, pushed her hair back and wiped her tears with his thumb.

"You know what Mom would say right now, don't you?" James asked.

Elizabeth nodded. "There's always tomorrow."

"And she'd be right," James suggested.

"So what about today?" Elizabeth asked between sniffles.

"Well, I guess the first priority is letting the others know," James said. "I'm not looking forward to that."

"How will you tell them? You can't really wait until you get everyone together, can you?" Elizabeth asked.

"No, I think it will be best to tell them individually," James agreed.

"And how do you think they will deal with it?" Elizabeth asked.

"Oh, I'm sure it will be like most other things. Mary will look for someone to blame and then she'll calm down and be just fine. I'm sure Anna will be her practical self. Rachel will fall-apart and think it was her fault.

And who knows how Thomas will react. Anyway, I'll have to pin him down first."

"They're lucky to have you for a brother James Cooper," Elizabeth said as she ran her fingers through her husband's thick hair. "You helped keep everyone together after your father died and I'm sure you'll do it this time too."

"Yes, but I had Mom's help last time," he said.

Elizabeth smiled. "I'll bet you still do."

James stood up and put the rocking chair back in its place by the Christmas tree. "I suppose I'd better get moving. I've got some phone calls to make."

"Jessica will be home from school in a little while. Do you think we should tell her when she gets here, or wait until the others come home?" Elizabeth asked.

"I think we should wait. A few hours won't make that much difference," James said.

"How are you going to tell them?" she asked.

"I'm not sure," James said. "Lisa and Allen are old enough to remember when Dad died, but Jessica was only two at the time. It will probably be a difficult concept for her to understand. That's another reason I want to wait and tell all of them together. It'll give me time to figure something out."

"I'll go make some lunch while you call your family," Elizabeth said.

"Maybe I'll feel like eating by then," James suggested as he walked down the hallway to the master bedroom.

Elizabeth was working in the kitchen when Jessica arrived home from kindergarten.

"Why is Daddy's car here?" she asked as she came through the front door.

"Because Daddy's here, silly," Elizabeth responded.

"Is he sick?"

"Sort of," Elizabeth said.

"Did you give him a note so he could come home?" Jessica asked.

"No, he didn't need a note. He just came home early because he has some things to do. Now why don't you put your boots and hat away, then you can eat your sandwich before I help you with your homework."

When James hadn't emerged from the bedroom after more than an hour, Elizabeth left Jessica drawing a picture and went back to check on him. He was lying on the bed staring at the ceiling.

"What are you doing?" she asked. "I thought you were going to call your family."

"Would you believe I couldn't reach any of them?" James answered.

"So I guess you can call them later," Elizabeth suggested.

James shrugged. "I left a message on Mary's and Anna's answering machines, so I'm sure I'll hear from them tonight."

"What about the others?" she asked.

"I just remembered that Rachel and Andrew are on their way back from his parent's place. They won't be home until tomorrow sometime," he said.

"And Thomas?" asked Elizabeth.

"I'll just have to keep trying and hope I'm lucky enough to track him down," James said.

"So what have you been doing all this time?" she asked.

"Thinking about Mom and how different our lives will be without her. She did so much that we just took for granted."

"That's what mothers do," Elizabeth pointed out.

James nodded and smiled. "I remember once in junior high school when I procrastinated reading Huck Finn for my literature class. There was a book report due the next day. I complained about being too tired to read, so Mom stayed up most of the night and read the book to me. Then she helped me write the report. She sent me to lie down for a while before school started. When I got up, I found that Mom had stayed up and fixed breakfast for everyone."

James paused, then said, "She was so tired when we got home from school that she could hardly keep her eyes open, but she still made our dinner and got us all settled for the night. She didn't complain about the lack of sleep and there was no lecture on the evils of procrastination. The guilt I felt after seeing what I had put her through was more searing than any lecture."

"She was amazing, that's for sure." Elizabeth turned to leave the room. "Come on," she said, "Jessica's been asking about you."

James followed Elizabeth to the kitchen.

"Hi Daddy," Jessica said. "I'm coloring."

"That's lovely sweetheart. How was school?"

"Fine. Mommy says you're sorta sick. Are you?" Jessica asked without lifting her eyes from her work.

"Let's just say I don't feel well," James replied.

Satisfied with the response, Jessica continued with her project.

Elizabeth handed James the sandwich she had prepared for him earlier. As he ate, he quizzed Jessica about her day and patiently listened to her minute-by-minute rundown.

"Here come the others," Elizabeth said, interrupting the father-daughter conversation.

Lisa and Allen could be heard from outside as they approached the front door.

"Mom!" Lisa called.

"In here," Elizabeth answered.

"Allen hit me with a snowball," Lisa protested as she entered the house.

"I wasn't throwing it at you," Allen offered in his own defense as he came in behind Lisa.

"Allen, tell your sister you're sorry, then both of you stop it please," James called from the kitchen.

Both children were silent. It was unusual for their father to be home when they arrived from school. They walked sheepishly into the kitchen.

"Hi Dad," Allen finally said. "Why are you home so early?"

James didn't respond.

Elizabeth broke the uncomfortable silence. "Kids, Dad and I need to talk to you."

Elizabeth directed the children to the front room and seated Lisa and Allen on the sofa. She sat down between them and boosted Jessica onto her lap. James took his place in the rocking chair.

"Children, I'm afraid I have some sad news about

Grandma." James spoke without emotion as he continued. "Something went wrong on her trip and she was hurt very badly."

"What happened?" Allen asked.

"We're not exactly sure, but apparently she was robbed and in the process, the robber shot her," James explained.

Lisa's lower lip started to quiver. "She's okay isn't she?"

James took in a deep breath. "I'm afraid she died," he said.

Allen's eyes filled with tears and Lisa began to openly sob. Elizabeth put an arm around each of them and pulled them toward Jessica.

Jessica's face remained expressionless. "Grandma's gone?" she asked.

"That's right, Jessica." James confirmed.

"Will she be back for our Christmas party?" Jessica inquired.

"I'm afraid not, Sweetie," Elizabeth answered.

Jessica looked puzzled, then asked, "Where did she go?"

"She went to be with Grandpa Paul," James replied.

"That's why you don't feel well, huh Daddy?" Jessica suggested.

James nodded, but didn't say a word.

CHAPTER SIX

"There's a message from James," Mary said as John entered the bedroom after tucking the children into bed.

"What did he say?" John asked.

"He just said to call him."

"Then call him," John suggested.

James and Mary frequently talked to each other over the telephone, but he rarely, if ever, left a message when she wasn't home. Mary sensed that something must be wrong. She sat on the edge of her bed and stared at the telephone.

John walked to the other side of the bed and pulled a book from his bedside table. He positioned himself behind Mary. "What's wrong?" he asked.

"Nothing," Mary unconvincingly replied. She picked up the telephone and dialed James' number.

"Hello," James said.

"Your message sounded urgent," Mary said. She silently waited for James to respond.

"Mary?" James asked.

"It's about Mom, isn't it?" Mary asked.

"I don't know how to tell you this..."

"I knew something was going to happen. So what is it, is she sick?" Mary asked. "I suppose they'll need to send a helicopter to get her off the ship."

"I wish it was that simple," James replied.

"What do you mean?" she asked. Mary's gut feeling

changed from simple concern to downright fear as she anticipated James' response. She reached behind her and took hold of John's hand.

"Mary, Mom was found dead in San Juan last night. She'd been shot," James said.

A cold chill spread through Mary's entire body. It was so real that John could feel it through her grasp. He placed the book he was reading face down on the bed, wrapped his arm around Mary's waist and listened to her side of the conversation.

"Mary?" James said after a prolonged pause.

"Shot? San Juan?" Mary asked. "How could that be? Wasn't she supposed to be on the ship?"

"Yes, she was," James responded. "But I guess she didn't make it. No one knows for sure what happened, but it looks like she was taken from the airport into San Juan and robbed."

"Can't the cruise company keep its passengers from being robbed?" Mary angrily asked.

"I don't think this could be helped," James said. "The police think Mom was lured away from the airport."

"Yeah, but they could have at least let us know when she didn't make it to the ship."

"Mary, they have thousands of passengers," James said calmly. "I'm sure dozens don't make it to the ship for one reason or another. Besides, what difference would it have made? Mom was probably already . . ." James paused.

"Dead," Mary offered, her volume increasing with each word she spoke. "How can you be so cold?"

"What do you mean, cold? This is my mother too. Do

you think I'm enjoying this?" James asked.

John squeezed Mary's hand as a signal to calm down.

"I'm sorry James, but do you have to say it?" she asked in a more relaxed tone.

"What do you want me to say Mary?" James asked.

"I don't know," Mary responded.

"Call it what you want, but Mom is just as dead," James said. "Anyway, we can't change what has happened."

"But if someone . . ."

"If someone what?" James said cutting Mary off mid-sentence, "would have held Mom's hand for the entire trip. Mary, quit trying to find someone to blame. Mom is gone, nothing will change that."

"I suppose you're right," Mary admitted after several moments of silence. "I just wish things would occasionally go as planned."

"They do, but usually not according to our plan." James said. "I'm sorry I had to give you this news, but now we just need to move ahead. Remember what we were taught?"

"I know, there's always tomorrow," Mary responded.

Feeling that his point had been made, James changed the direction of the conversation. "I haven't been able to reach any of the others yet. Rachel and Andrew are still out of town and Anna hasn't been home. Anyway, I think I'll just talk to Anna then let her tell Rachel, unless you want to do it."

"I think Anna's the perfect choice," Mary said. "So what about Thomas?"

"I'm working on it," James assured. "After we let the

others know, we'll need to get together to make some decisions."

"So much for Sunday's Christmas party. In fact, so much for Christmas," Mary scornfully replied.

"What are you talking about, Mary?" James asked. "Do you really think Mom would want us to let this ruin our holidays? She loved Christmas, and there's no reason for us not to carry on with our plans. Besides, we owe it to our kids to make this Christmas as normal as possible, otherwise, they'll never enjoy this time of year again."

John remained quiet as Mary listened. He knew he didn't need to respond to Mary's outburst, since James was well versed at doing so.

Mary sighed. "I'll wait to hear from you then. Good-bye, James . . . and thanks," she said. She hung up the telephone and sat in silence.

John reached over and put his other arm around Mary.

"I guess you heard," Mary said. Her eyes were fixed straight ahead.

"Enough," John replied. "Do you want to talk?"

"I'm not sure what I want," she said as tears began streaming down her face. The droplets flowed over her cheeks and fell onto John's hand.

John pulled Mary closer and embraced her from behind. "It's hard to know what to say at a time like this," he whispered into her ear.

"Just say everything will be all right," Mary requested.

"You know it will," John said.

"It doesn't seem fair," Mary complained. "Things were finally starting to get back to normal for Mom after Dad died."

John began stroking Mary's long chestnut hair as she spoke.

"As much as it scared me, I knew this trip would be good for her. She was supposed to find her independence. And what did she find?"

"Her independence," John offered.

Mary contemplated John's comment. Turning and resting the side of her head against his chest, she looked up at John and smiled in agreement.

"I didn't even ask James when it happened," Mary commented between sniffles.

"It doesn't really matter, does it?" John asked as he handed her a tissue.

"I guess not," Mary responded.

"Do you think the kids will understand?" John asked.

"Not until they realize Grandma isn't coming around anymore. They sure will miss their Thursday trips to the park with her."

John nodded in agreement.

Mary sat forward and looked into John's eyes. "Do you know what I liked best about taking the kids to the park with Mom?" she asked.

"No, what?" John inquired.

"It reminded me of when I was a little girl and Mom used to take me to the park." Mary laid her head back on John's chest as she continued. "She could push me higher than any mom there. I especially loved it when she would pull me back as far as she could, then run and push me forward over her head and come out in front of me. I knew she was the only person in the whole world who could do such a thing. I would laugh so hard I'd almost lose my grip on the chains. Mom would reach out and I'd fall forward into her arms as I swung forward toward her."

"And I thought you were going to the park for the boys," John teased.

"Mostly for them, but some for me too," Mary admitted. "You know, it's funny," she continued, "the swings are all I remember about the park when I was young. I wonder if that's significant?"

"Sure it is," John said confidently. "It proves your mother understood that the simple things are what count."

"Why is it that you learn the most from your parents when you're parents yourself?" Mary asked.

"I believe it's called maturity." John replied.

John and Mary sat quietly as they contemplated how their lives had just changed.

Mary broke the silence. "You'd better go to bed so you'll be ready for work in the morning."

"I'm happy to sit here and talk if you need me to," John replied.

"You go ahead, I'll be fine," Mary assured.

John released his embrace and got off the bed. He changed into his pajamas as Mary sat in quiet reflection. "Are you going to join me?" he asked.

"This is the sort of thing that always happens to someone else," Mary said without acknowledging John's question. "You hear about tragic events but never imagine that someday someone will be talking about a tragedy that occurred in your life."

"I'm sure everyone who goes through something like this feels the same way," John suggested.

"Do you think so?" Mary asked. "Do you really think that everyone goes through life assuming a natural immunity to heartrending events? Or do some people have a sense that they will one-day face a real calamity?"

John climbed under the covers on his side of the bed and stared blankly at Mary. "What's your point?" he asked in confusion.

"My point is, I never dreamed that my mother's life would come to a tragic end. Oh I realized she could go suddenly like Dad, but never like this."

"Does the way a person dies make any difference?" John asked.

Mary thought for a moment before answering. "Probably not much to the person who experiences death, but I think it makes a big difference to those left behind."

John sat up in preparation for what he knew could be a lengthy conversation. He adjusted his pillow so it would support his back against the headboard. "How so?" he asked.

"Think about it," she said. "If James had just called and told me Mother had been shot by the police while trying to rob a convenience store, don't you think you'd feel a little different right now?"

"I'm sure I would," John agreed.

"And what if we were informed that she had jumped in front of a bullet in order to save the life of a child?"

"Okay, but in either case, your mother is still gone," John said. "The loss is just as real, regardless of the cause."

"But John, I don't want to always think of my mother staring down the barrel of a gun in absolute fear. She died alone. At least Dad had most of his family with him."

John began to nod in understanding. "So if your mother had died while saving someone's life, even if she was alone, you would associate her death with that act of love. But since she died in a strange place under what were probably very difficult circumstances, your thoughts will focus on the tragedy."

Mary started to cry again. "I don't want to always be plagued by thoughts of Mom's terror."

John moved closer to Mary and took her in his arms. He took a tissue and wiped her eyes. "It doesn't have to be that way," he assured. "Your mother lived a wonderful life and built a real legacy for her family. Think about how she lived, not how she died."

"But it's so hard," Mary protested.

"I know it's hard right now, but it will get easier."

"How do you know?" Mary asked.

"Because your mother spent most of her life giving to her husband and children. One incident, no matter how terrible, can't possibly overshadow all of that."

Mary smiled through the tears and snuggled closer to John. "No wonder Mom liked you better than me," she said.

CHAPTER SEVEN

"Excuse me a moment." Anna smiled as she stood up. She left her customers contemplating their choices and walked behind the counter to the telephone. "Lyn Jewelers. This is Anna," she answered.

"Hi Sis," James said. "Is this a good time?" His voice was solemn and faint.

"Actually, I'm with some customers, but I should be done soon. Is it okay if I call you in a few minutes?"

"That will be fine. I'm at home. I'll talk to you in a little while."

"Great," Anna said. "Good bye." She hung up the telephone and returned to the table where the young couple was considering the purchase of an engagement ring.

"I really like this one," the young woman said as she held up her left hand seeking Anna's approval.

"It looks gorgeous on you," Anna assured. "What do you think?" she asked the young man.

He fidgeted in his seat before responding. "Um, yeah," he said hesitantly, "It looks good."

"You know," Anna said as she picked up a less expensive ring, "this one is beautiful too." She caught the young man's eye and winked as she switched the rings on the girl's finger. "Oh, now that is stunning."

The young man smiled. "I really like that one," he said without hesitation.

"Do you think so?" the young woman asked.

"Look at how the band enhances the contour of your finger. And the cut of that diamond is perfect for your hands," Anna said with enthusiasm.

"I think you're right. We'll take this one," the young woman said.

Anna smiled in approval of their decision. She accompanied the young man to the counter where the transaction was completed.

"Congratulations you two," Anna said, "and Merry Christmas."

"Thanks," the young man said. "You have a Merry Christmas too."

The excited young couple left the store hand-in-hand and giggling.

Anna returned to the telephone and dialed James' number.

"Hello," Elizabeth answered.

"Hi Elizabeth. How are you?" Anna asked.

"I'm fine, thank you."

"And how are the kids?" Anna asked.

"They're fine too," Elizabeth said.

"Great! And how's that Christmas baking coming along?" Anna asked.

"I guess your calling for James?" Elizabeth said without regard to Anna's question.

"Yes, I'm returning his call."

"Just a minute, I'll get him," Elizabeth said.

Anna was surprised about Elizabeth's obvious preoccupation, but assumed that she must have been in the middle of something. She hummed "Silent Night" quietly while she waited for James to come to the telephone.

"Hello Anna," James said.

"Listen, I'm sorry I didn't call you back last night, but I spent the day at a trade show for Mr. Lyn and it was after midnight when I got home," Anna explained.

"That's fine," James assured.

"I know, but then I didn't call you this morning either. I got in so late last night that I overslept and had to rush to make it here on time."

"Really Anna, I understand," James insisted.

"Well, thank you for being so tolerant. So what can I do for you?" she asked.

"Anna, I got a call from the Police Department yesterday morning. They had just been notified that Mom was found dead in an alley in San Juan Tuesday morning."

Anna gasped and put her free hand over her mouth. "What happened?" she asked in disbelief.

"Of course no one knows for sure, but it looks like she was taken into town, robbed, and shot. She never made it to the cruise ship."

"I can't believe it. She was supposed to be home for Christmas," Anna said. Tears began to run down her cheeks and onto her blouse. "I don't know what to say."

"There isn't really anything to say," James assured. "I've spoken with Mary and hope to talk to Thomas this afternoon. Rachel should be getting back soon and I wondered if you would mind telling her."

"No, I don't mind. In fact, I think that's probably a

good idea," Anna agreed. She took a handkerchief from her skirt pocket and wiped her eyes.

"We all need to meet and discuss a few things. I'll organize a time and place and let you know," James said. "The police chief said he'll share any new information as soon as he gets it, so hopefully we'll have some better direction by the time we meet."

"James, sometimes I wonder what we'd do without you," Anna suggested.

"I'm sure you'd get by," James responded.

"I'm not so sure. How are you going to find the prodigal son anyway?" Anna asked.

"I have a pretty good idea where to find him," James answered.

"Well, good luck," Anna said. "Keep me informed."

"I will," James said. "Good bye"

Anna hung up the telephone and sat down on the stool behind the counter. She placed her elbow on the glass top and rested her chin in her hand. Her forearm became moist as the tears rolled from her cheeks and splattered on the countertop. Anna was grateful that there were no customers present to see her in such a state.

"What's wrong Anna?" Mr. Lyn asked as he emerged from the back of the store. The elderly gentleman walked to the front of the counter, took the hanky from Anna's hand and wiped her tears. His jeweler's loupe was still lowered in front of his eye.

Anna looked up and feigned a smile. "Just a minor family crisis Mr. Lyn," she responded.

"Anything I can do?" Mr. Lyn asked as he looked into

Anna's eyes. His concern was genuine and his offer sincere.

Anna had grown very attached to her aging employer. She had worked for him since she graduated from college two years earlier. His conventional wisdom reminded Anna of her father. His friendship had helped her through the difficult time of her twin sister's marriage. While Anna and Rachel still had an unbreakable bond with each other, Anna recognized that Andrew had become Rachel's new best friend: and appropriately so.

Anna reached up and raised the jeweler's loupe on her boss's glasses. "Mr. Lyn, that was my older brother on the phone. He was calling to tell me that my mother was killed in San Juan."

"Oh dear," he said. "I'm so sorry."

"You know, it's funny," Anna mused. "Even after my father died, I never gave any thought to the fact that Mom was going to die someday. I just sort of figured she'd be around forever, doing what she always did."

"I only met her a time or two, but she sure seemed like a fine woman," Mr. Lyn said.

"Yes, she was. Even when times got tough, she was always looking at the bright side of things. The last few years have been kind of rough on her. First Dad died then my younger brother sort of went off the deep-end. I thought of this cruise as kind of a reward for her valiant efforts to keep going. Some reward, huh?"

"I think she's received the best reward available," Mr. Lyn suggested.

"What do you mean?" Anna asked. She took her

handkerchief from Mr. Lyn's hand and wiped her eyes again.

"She's back with your father and doesn't have to worry about the day-to-day problems we're still facing. What could be better than that?"

"You're right. Most of us would appreciate that wouldn't we?" Anna agreed.

"Anna, why don't you take the rest of the day off?" Mr. Lyn offered.

"No," Anna replied, "you need me to watch the front so you can spend time figuring out your new rolling mill."

"Anna, that's just an excuse," Mr. Lyn wisely returned. "You know there is someone coming after Christmas to help me with the rolling mill."

"Yeah, but until then . . ."

"Anna, I'm caught up enough until then," Mr. Lyn interrupted.

"I do appreciate the offer, Mr. Lyn, but I really think I'll do better here at work than I would at home on my own," Anna responded.

"What about your brothers or sisters?" he asked.

"They need time to themselves with their families," Anna reasoned. "Maybe I could just take an early extended lunch break."

"You take whatever time you need," Mr. Lyn said. "And you just let me know if you change your mind about going home early."

"Thank you. You're such a sweetheart," she said. Anna turned and passed through the red velvet curtain that separated the showroom and front counter from the rest of the shop. She walked past Mr. Lyn's workbench along the narrow passage that led to a small break-room at the back. Closing the door behind her, she moved a chair away from the small round table in the middle of the room and placed it near the telephone on the wall.

Anna sat silently for several minutes. The tears had stopped and she knew she had practical issues to deal with. "Putting it off won't make it any easier," she said aloud.

She picked up the telephone and dialed Rachel's number. After several rings, she hung up. "Just as well you're not home, because I'm still not sure how I'm going to break the news," Anna said as if Rachel were in the room with her.

Leaning her head against the wall, Anna allowed her mind to travel to another moment in time. She and Rachel celebrated their 21st birthday with their parents a few months before their father's death. The two college-girls were treated to a formal evening complete with dinner and dancing. Their father joked about being the luckiest man on earth that evening because he could dance with three beautiful women and none of them would be jealous. Anna reflected on a conversation she had with her mother that evening while Rachel was dancing with their father.

"You know she needs you, don't you?"

"Who?" Anna asked.

"Rachel. She would have a hard time if it weren't for you," Martha observed.

"I don't understand," Anna said.

"We're all born with needs that make us depend on other people. But I'm not talking about the kind of dependence a baby has on its parents."

"So what are you talking about?" Anna asked.

"There's a deeper need inside all of us and it changes with the different stages in our lives. I think the Lord must have designed it that way to remind us that we can't go through life alone," Martha explained. "We have to depend on others and allow others to depend on us."

"Okay," Anna agreed. "But what does that have to do with Rachel and me?"

"Well, I think you two were born twins to compliment each other. Rachel needs . . . boosting every now and then, and you're a good booster."

"I don't do any more than anyone else would do for her," Anna suggested.

"Yes you do Anna. You just aren't aware of it because it comes so naturally to you," Martha said. "You defend her, you encourage her . . ."

"I love her, Mom," Anna interrupted. "What else should I do?"

"Nothing more. I just want you to realize that right now she needs you. But there will come a time when someone else will meet her current need," Martha cautioned.

"You mean when she marries Andrew?" Anna stated.

"Andrew or someone else," Martha corrected. "And when it happens, I don't want you to feel like Rachel loves you any less. Besides, she'll still need you for some things."

"You're talking like you know she'll get married before me," Anna observed.

Martha validated Anna's observation with a wink and a smile.

"You said Rachel and I compliment each other?" Anna queried.

"Right," Martha confirmed.

"So what need of mine do you see Rachel meeting and what happens to it when she gets married?"

"Your need is to get her there," Martha said. "Then someone will come along that will be able to meet a newly discovered need within you."

"I hope he's like Dad," Anna said.

"Me too," Martha concurred.

Anna was startled by a ringing telephone. She knew Mr. Lyn was watching the front of the store so she disregarded the sound until it stopped. The steady light next to the button labeled line-one indicated that Mr. Lyn had answered it.

Reaching above her head, Anna pushed the button labeled line-two, picked up the handset and dialed Rachel's telephone number.

CHAPTER EIGHT

"Is that the telephone?" Rachel asked as she opened the car door.

"I think it is," Andrew replied.

"I'll get it," Rachel said as she ran up the front steps of the house. Inserting the key into the lock, she turned it and opened the door. She sprinted across the front room to the telephone and picked up the receiver. "Hello," she panted.

"Are you okay?" Anna asked.

"Yeah, we just got home and I had to run in from outside," Rachel said, "but I'm fine."

"Did you have a nice trip?" Anna asked.

"Are you referring to our vacation or my stumble as I ran for the phone?" Rachel jested.

"The vacation," Anna replied soberly.

"It was very nice, thank you." Rachel was confused by Anna's apparent but unusual disregard for her witty comment. "So to what do I owe the pleasure of a midday telephone call from my twin sister?" she asked curiously.

"I was wondering if I could come over in a few minutes and talk to you and Andrew," Anna said. "I'm just getting off for lunch."

"You know you're always welcome to come over, but why the urgency?" Rachel asked.

"We just need to talk," Anna said.

Rachel sat silently. She was taken aback by Anna's

curious request and was not sure how to respond.

"Well, is it all right if I come?" Anna asked.

Rachel continued in silent contemplation for several seconds before responding. "Anna, we'd love to see you, but why don't you just tell me what's going on?"

Andrew came in from outside and sat on the suitcases he had toted in with him. "Who is it?" he whispered.

Rachel covered the mouthpiece. "It's Anna," she said while shaking her head in disapproval of his interruption.

"I think it would be best if we talked about it when I get there," Anna replied.

Rachel began to feel frightened. From the time they were little girls, she and Anna had been unable to hide their feelings from each other. She sensed that something was terribly wrong.

"Anna, I know you're just thinking of my feelings," Rachel said," but there's something bad you need to tell me. Don't torture me by making me wait until you can get here."

Anna said nothing.

"Anna, please. Just tell me what's wrong," Rachel insisted.

"Rachel . . ." Anna paused. She cleared her throat then continued. "Rachel, Mom's dead."

Rachel dropped the telephone as she fell back against the wall and slowly slid down until she was sitting on the floor. She drew her knees up to her chest and covered her face with her open hands. "No! She can't be!" she sobbed.

Andrew knelt in front of Rachel and put his arm around her shoulder. He picked up the telephone. "Anna, what's going on?" he asked abruptly.

"Andrew, I'm sorry. I wanted to come over and tell both of you together, but Rachel insisted that I tell her now," Anna explained.

"Tell her what?" Andrew asked.

"James called me this morning and told me Mom was found dead in Puerto Rico on Tuesday. The police think she was probably lured away from the airport, taken to the city, robbed, and shot."

Andrew sat next to Rachel and pulled her close to his side. "That's it?" he asked.

"That's about all we know right now," Anna said. "James said the Police Department will update us when they hear more."

"I guess the others know?" Andrew asked.

"James spoke with Mary yesterday and hopes to get with Thomas later today," Anna replied.

"Is there anything we need to do?" Andrew asked.

"James is trying to organize a meeting with the others so we can discuss things. He'll let us know where and when after he talks with Thomas. Until then, just take care of my sister."

"Sure thing. I guess we'll just wait to hear from you then," Andrew said.

"Tell Rachel I'll call her later," Anna said.

"Okay, good-bye," Andrew responded. He hung up the telephone and embraced Rachel with both arms.

Rachel wrapped her arms around Andrew's waist and rested her head against his chest.

"It's okay, honey," Andrew assured as he caressed the back of her head.

"I shouldn't have done it," Rachel said between sobs. "Why did I do it?"

"Do what?" Andrew queried.

"Let her go." Rachel replied.

"Huh?" Andrew had no idea what Rachel was talking about.

"When Mom came over last week she said she had decided not to go on the cruise.

She said it was too close to Christmas. We talked for hours and I finally convinced her she needed to do it," Rachel explained.

"Oh Rachel. This isn't your fault. You had no way of knowing," Andrew assured. He took a box of tissues from the bookshelf and offered it to her.

"No, but maybe Mom had a feeling that something bad was going to happen," Rachel argued. She took a tissue from the box and wiped her eyes before continuing. "All our lives Mom and Dad taught us to follow those silent promptings. 'Use the gift God has given you,' they would say. 'Do what you feel deep inside, not necessarily what logic would have you do.' What right did I have to talk Mom into doing something she was unsure about?"

"Don't you think your mother practiced what she preached? I'm sure she did what she felt she needed to do. All you did was reassure her that her decision was right," Andrew replied.

"When she came to me, her decision was to stay home. I used logic to convince her she needed to go."

"And she agreed with you. Rachel, what did you tell her?" Andrew inquired.

"I told her the trip would be good for her," she responded.

"And why did you tell her that?" Andrew asked.

"Because I felt it would be."

"Exactly. You did what you felt deep inside, didn't you?"

Rachel lifted her head from Andrew's chest and lowered her eyes to the ground. "Maybe you're right," she admitted. She turned her face towards Andrew and looked into his eyes. "But why would I feel good about the wrong thing?"

"Who said it was the wrong thing? You're assuming she wasn't supposed to die. Do you really think it's a good idea to question God and his motives?" Andrew asked.

"I'm not questioning Him. I just don't understand why bad things have to happen to good people," Rachel said.

"How else would we learn anything?" Andrew asked.

"What do you mean?" Rachel questioned.

"I mean it's the trials in life that make us strong. God knows that, your parents knew that, and I think you know it too," Andrew suggested. He placed his hand on Rachel's abdomen. "You won't deny our little one all of life's lessons will you?"

"No, I guess not," Rachel said.

"And wasn't it your father who always said he learned more from the 'School of Hard Knocks' than he ever learned in college?"

Rachel nodded and placed her head back on Andrew's chest.

"We didn't even get to tell her our news," Rachel lamented.

"No, we didn't, but I'll bet she knows," Andrew said as he took a tissue and wiped the tears from Rachel's eyes.

"How do you feel about Martha as a middle name for our baby?" Rachel asked.

Andrew chuckled. "Just fine unless we have a boy!"

Rachel smiled and shook her head. "Isn't it ironic? One minute life is giving us cause to celebrate, and the next minute it's causing us to mourn. I'm thrilled about being pregnant, yet at the same time I almost feel guilty about it."

"I wish you'd stop feeling guilty about everything," Andrew jested.

"You know what I mean," Rachel said. "I was looking forward to seeing my family at our Christmas dinner so we could share our news and now we'll have to keep the excitement inside. It's not going to be easy. Everyone will wonder why I seem so happy."

"I suppose it would have been easier if we'd found out about the baby next week," Andrew agreed. "But that's not the way it happened and now we have to deal with it. Besides, it's Christmas. People are supposed to be happy."

"When do you think we should tell them I'm expecting?" Rachel asked.

"I don't know. Just tell them when it feels right I guess." Andrew moved his arm from Rachel's waist and stood up. "There's nothing wrong with being happy about one thing and sad about something else at the same time," he said.

Rachel lifted her hands and waited for Andrew to help her to her feet. He helped her stand, then picked up the suitcases.

"I think I'll unpack later," Rachel called after Andrew as he made his way to the bedroom. She turned to the bookshelf and lifted down a large photo album. Sitting on the sofa, she placed the book on her lap and opened it to the first page. Tears filled her eyes again as she viewed a photograph of her and Anna in the arms of their mother. The caption indicated that Rachel and Anna were only one week old when the photo was taken. "Oh mother, I wish you could be here to take a picture of me holding my baby," she said aloud.

As she turned the pages of the album, Rachel felt like she was turning pages in her life. The first pages had pictures of her and Anna with their parents and James and Mary. Later, Thomas began appearing with the others. There were a few pictures with Elizabeth and John and of course several with Andrew. Then her father was no longer there. Now her mother too, would disappear from the album as new pages were filled.

"What are you doing?" Andrew asked, interrupting her reverie. He gazed at the open book.

"Just thinking about the new void that will be here now that Mom's gone," Rachel said turning to a blank page. "I wish I could simply turn back a few pages and have her here again."

"You're still trying to blame yourself aren't you?" he asked.

"No!" Rachel insisted. She looked up at Andrew and his questioning eyes. "I don't know," she conceded.

"Yesterday's gone Rachel and today's quickly fading. But there's . . ."

". . . always tomorrow," Rachel said cutting Andrew short.

"And tomorrow there will be someone to fill that void," Andrew added. "Your mother loved her grand-children and I'm sure it would make her proud to know that another one is taking her spot in our photo album. It was the same with your father and Mary's kids. That's how life works. People die and others are born to take their place."

"You make it sound so matter-of-fact," Rachel protested.

Andrew nodded. "It is matter-of-fact."

CHAPTER NINE

"Thomas, I know you're in there. Open the door." James' voice could be heard from outside.

Thomas rolled over and put a pillow over his head in an attempt to block out the sound. Soon the knocking started again. He removed the pillow, sat up and dropped his feet over the edge of the bed onto the bare floor. Slowly he stood and dragged himself across the room. He undid the latch and opened the door. Without looking at James or saying a word, he slumped into the ragged chair situated next to the door. He pushed his uncombed shoulder-length hair off his face.

"Where have you been?" James asked tersely. He walked into the two-room apartment and took a folding chair from beside the card-table that was the only other piece of furniture in the room. James sat down directly in front of Thomas and glared into his eyes.

"What difference does it make?" Thomas responded.

"It makes a lot of difference. I've been trying to get hold of you since yesterday. What time did you get in last night; or should I say this morning?"

"Look, I don't have to take this abuse. And what gives you the right to expect a daily accounting of my life?" Thomas asked.

"Perhaps the fact that I'm paying your rent at the moment. I told you I'm only going to help as long as you show some initiative and look for another job. I don't consider staying out all night a responsible act." James replied.

"Okay, so I was out a little late, what's the harm?"

"Oh, maybe that half your day has been spent in bed instead of out job hunting." James said.

"All right, I'm sorry," Thomas said insincerely. "So is that the only reason you came over; to wake me up and lecture me?"

"Actually, I wish it was," James replied. "But I'm afraid I have some bad news. It's about Mom."

"What did she do, wreck her car again?" Thomas asked sarcastically.

"It's a little more serious than that Thomas." James stood up and walked to the kitchen sink and the only window in the room. He peered through the dirty glass as though he was concentrating on something outside, but the red brick wall of the neighboring building was the only visible scenery.

"Well, are you going to tell me or not?" Thomas asked.

James turned and leaned against the counter in front of the sink. "Thomas, I know you and Mom haven't seen eye-to-eye since Dad died, but I think it's time to put those feelings aside."

"Oh, I get it," Thomas said angrily. "She sent you here didn't she? I suppose you're going to tell me that she's sick and nearly on her deathbed. Then I'm supposed to go home, beg for her forgiveness and tell her how much I'm looking forward to spending Christmas with the family. Is that it? Well you can forget it and so can she." Thomas turned sideways in the chair, flung his legs over one side and folded his arms across his bare chest.

"Nobody . . ."

Thomas continued his monologue, interrupting James' attempt to speak. "That's the problem with this family. Everyone has my life all mapped-out. I'm expected to do what they want so they can be happy. Nobody cares about what I want. And what about your promise to me?"

"I've kept my promise," James assured. "Nobody knows where you are except me." James walked back to the metal chair and sat down. He leaned forward and rested his arms on his knees. His fingers were intertwined and his eyes were directed at Thomas.

Thomas was silent, but turned his head and looked into James' expressionless face. "All right then, what have you come to tell me?"

James drew in a deep breath and let it escape slowly before answering. "Sometimes you know you should do something, but put it off while waiting for the right time. Of course, you run the risk of putting it off until it's too late."

Thomas leaned his head back and rolled his eyes. "I'm getting another lecture aren't I?"

James ignored the question and continued. "But sometimes, even when it seems too late, you can still make things right."

"Aside from the fact that you think I need to make up with Mom, what's your point?"

"You knew Mom left for her cruise?" James asked.

"Yeah, so what?"

"She ran into some problems in Puerto Rico and won't be home on Sunday as expected," James explained.

Thomas just smiled and shrugged his shoulders as if unconcerned.

"Thomas, Mom was found dead on Tuesday."

The smile on Thomas' lips disappeared and the color drained from his face. He tried to swallow the lump in his throat, but it wouldn't move. A sudden chill permeated his body as if he'd stepped outside into the winter air. He clenched his jaw and began breathing audibly deeper.

James extended his hand toward Thomas, but Thomas pushed it away.

"Is that all you came to tell me?" Thomas asked coldly.

"I guess it is," James replied. "And that the girls are meeting at my house tomorrow to discuss what we need to do. We'd love to have you there. We need you there."

"Yeah, I'll see," Thomas responded. His eyes appeared glazed and were fixed straight ahead.

"Is one o'clock a good time for you?" James asked.

"Yeah, whatever," was Thomas' monotone reply.

"I guess I'll be going now." James stood and returned his chair to its original position at the table. As he walked toward the door, he reached into his coat pocket and pulled out an envelope. "Here," he said handing Thomas the envelope. "This is for you."

Thomas took the envelope from James' hand without altering his gaze.

"Give me a call if you need to talk or anything," James offered.

Thomas nodded.

James opened the front door and stopped. He briefly put his hand on Thomas' shoulder, then stepped into the hallway, closing the door behind him.

Thomas sat in a state of confused disbelief for several minutes after James left. Righting himself in the chair, he placed his feet on the floor and began to examine the white, letter-sized envelope in his hand. It was addressed to him in his mother's handwriting. He opened it and withdrew the folded pages. He lifted the top fold and began to read:

Dearest Thomas,

For some time now, I have been hoping for the opportunity to speak with you and to share some of my feelings in person. As time has passed and the chances for such an opportunity appear less likely, I am putting these feelings into writing. I will leave this letter with James and will instruct him to give it to you if I die before having an opportunity to deliver its contents myself.

I want you to know that I have written and rewritten this letter more times than I can count. I'm just not sure of the best way to say what I want to say. I hope this final draft expresses my feelings in a way that will be meaningful to both of us.

Let me start by telling you that I love you. If you remember nothing else from this letter, please remember that I always have and always will love you.

Without a doubt, the hardest day of my life was the day your father died. I know that was a rough day for you as well. I think we both considered him our best friend. I knew I would miss his quiet nature, his dry sense of humor, his humble wisdom, and his companionship.

You weren't there when he died, but I'm sure you know what his final words were. "There's always tomorrow," he said. As usual, he was right. Tomorrow followed and that day became yesterday. I didn't know, nor could I change what tomorrow would bring. But I could decide how to react. I could move ahead in the same direction, change course or simply give up.

Isn't it ironic that a few months later another man left my life and chose the same parting words, only he uttered them in derision? "When will you be back?" I asked. "There's always tomorrow," you scoffed.

To your father, "tomorrow" had no specific definition. It could mean an opportunity to do better, a chance to take a different road or the permission to try something new. "There's always tomorrow" was his answer to everything, but that's because in reality, it represented nothing more than never-ending hope. You blasted the words at me as though they meant nothing more than "who knows, but *maybe sometime."*

Thomas, I don't believe you intended to hurt me. I know you were confused. I'm sorry if you felt I was pressuring you to accept the basketball scholarship from the Community College. I confess that I was, but at the time, I couldn't see any other way for you to attend college. Your father's death brought a "tomorrow" with some challenges that we weren't prepared for. I'm sorry that I couldn't honor his promise to let you attend the school of your choice.

But all of that is yesterday, as is my life. So Thomas, look to tomorrow and see if there isn't room in your heart to forgive me. It isn't too late. Your brother and sisters love you and want you back as a part of their lives. They need you. Show your love for me by being part of the family once again.

Your father's words have helped me remember that though I may be without him for a few "todays," there will come a tomorrow, my tomorrow, when we'll be together again. Your words have left me with hope that though you may be away from the family for a few "todays," there will come a tomorrow, your tomorrow, when you'll be back.

My tomorrow has come. Maybe yours has too.

All my love forever,
Mother

CHAPTER TEN

James stood next to the Christmas tree by the large window in his front room. Separating the louvers on the aluminum blind, he peered through the opening at the car parked across the street. After an audible sigh, he released his hold on the blind allowing the slats to snap back into their horizontal position.

"Well, it's a quarter past. We might as well get started," James said to the room full of guests.

Mary, Anna and Rachel were seated next to each other on the sofa. John was in the rocking chair and Andrew sat on the floor with his back resting against Rachel's legs. James joined Elizabeth who was sitting on the piano bench. The room was quiet except for the laughter coming from the family room where the children were playing together.

"I guess I'll start by telling you about the conversation I had this morning with Chief Rosen," James said, breaking the increasingly uncomfortable silence.

"Wait!" Anna protested. "What about Thomas?"

"If he wanted to be here, he would be by now," Mary said as she folded her arms across her chest. "Let's just go ahead."

"I agree," Rachel said timidly. "Don't you?" she asked Andrew who just shrugged.

"Now hang on," James cautioned, "I think he'll come around, but he'll need our understanding."

"Oh, I understand perfectly," Mary said. "He walked out of our lives with no real explanation and we're supposed to welcome him back as if nothing ever happened."

"Mary," John said softly, "this isn't the time."

"Why isn't it the time?" she asked.

"Because we're here to talk about Mother," James responded.

"This is about Mother. Thomas left her at a time when she really needed him to be at home," Mary returned. "Did you ever consider the fact that she lost both Dad and Thomas within a few months of each other?"

"Mary," John said a little more sternly.

"Fine!" Mary said in disgust. "I'll keep quiet."

"We don't want you to keep quiet Mary. We need to work through this together," Anna said.

Mary nodded.

"I know it's frustrating, but let's not worry about Thomas right now," James suggested. He reached behind him and took a manila envelope from the top of the piano. Motioning to Elizabeth, he opened it and dumped the contents into her cupped hands.

"What's that?" Rachel asked.

"Chief Rosen gave them to me this morning," James answered. "This is what they found in Mom's purse."

"Why did we get that before Mom's body arrived?" Mary asked.

"The Chief said he requested it. I guess he was afraid it might get lost if they held it to send with the body. Anyway, he said he figured we'd want something as soon as possible," James explained.

"He sounds like a very nice man," Anna said.

James nodded in agreement. "He said he talked with the San Juan Police this morning and they will complete their investigation later tomorrow. With Monday being Christmas, he said we probably shouldn't expect her body to arrive until late Tuesday evening."

"Do we need to make funeral plans or anything?" Rachel asked.

"I called Mr. Price at Rosewood Funeral Home and he said it would be a good idea to discuss some of the basic things we want," James answered. "When her body arrives, he'll transport her from the airport and then meet with us to get the details."

"So what's Elizabeth holding?" Mary queried.

"Not much," James responded. "There's an I.D. card, a hanky, her compact, a cruise brochure, some loose change and a business card."

"What about her tickets or her pictures?" Mary asked.

James shook his head

"What's the business card?" Anna asked.

James picked up the card from Elizabeth's hand. "It's for a Joseph Watkins from Atlanta, Georgia."

"How do you think she got it?" Rachel asked.

"I wondered that too," James said. "I've been tempted to call the number on it and ask Mr. Watkins. What do you think?" He held the card up and then gave it back to Elizabeth.

"I think it's a good idea," Mary said.

"Me too," Rachel said. "What do think, Andrew?"

"Yeah," Andrew responded, "sounds good."

"He may have been one of the last people to see Mother alive," Anna suggested.

"I thought the same thing," Elizabeth rejoined.

"What else does the card have on it?" John asked.

Elizabeth turned the card over and perused it. "It just says that he's a sales rep. for this company."

"Does it say what he sells?" John asked.

"Nope," Elizabeth answered.

Everyone sat in quiet contemplation until Rachel began to sniffle. "You know, I've had a hard time believing Mom's really gone," she said. "I feel almost as if calling this Mr. Wa . . . whoever will make things better. Almost like he'll be able to say something that will console us."

"Like he's the key to something we should know," Anna added.

"Yeah," Rachel said, "exactly."

"I can't say I'd thought of it that way," Elizabeth said, "but I do think calling him might help."

"There must have been a reason she kept that card," Mary observed. "You know Mom; if something had no useful purpose, out it went."

John laughed. "You wouldn't by chance be thinking of a certain sweater would you?"

"As a matter of fact, I am," Mary confirmed.

Everyone in the room began to chuckle, except for Andrew. "Am I missing something?" he asked.

"No, it happened before we met," Rachel said.

"And...?" Andrew asked.

"When she was in high school, Mary let everyone

know she didn't think too much of dating because it involved boys," Rachel said. "By the time she started college, there wasn't a boy around who dared ask her out."

"Which was fine with me," Mary volunteered.

"Anyway," Rachel continued, "since John wasn't from around here, he didn't know she was 'untouchable' and asked her for a date."

"And that caught me off-guard," Mary said. "I was so shocked that I accepted his invitation without thinking."

John smiled. "It was really my good looks," he suggested.

Mary ignored the interruption and continued. "To my surprise, we hit it off and started dating regularly."

"But she didn't dare admit to Mom and Dad that she was seeing someone," Anna said.

"She was afraid it might ruin her image," Rachel interjected.

Anna continued. "And all of that was fine until John gave Mary his letterman's sweater to wear."

"Are you confused yet?" Rachel asked Andrew.

Andrew leaned his head back onto Rachel's lap and looked up at her. "I'm not sure," he answered, "keep going."

"Well, she knew Mom and Dad would suspect something if they saw her wearing the sweater, so she used to keep it hidden in the garage when she wasn't wearing it," Rachel explained. "But one day, Mom was looking for something in the garage and guess what she found?"

"The sweater," Andrew hypothesized.

"Yep," Mary said. "And guess what she did with it?"

"She must have gotten rid of it," Andrew said.

Mary smiled at Andrew, then at John and nodded. "She didn't know anyone named John and couldn't imagine how his college sweater ended up in our garage. So she gave it to the Salvation Army."

"Did it really take you a month to tell John what happened?" Elizabeth asked Mary.

"It did," Mary admitted.

"So how did you find out what happened?" Andrew asked.

"About a week after it disappeared, I finally got brave and asked Dad if he'd seen the sweater," Mary said. "Mom had shown it to him and asked if he knew where it came from before she gave it away."

"Did he say 'there's always tomorrow' somewhere in his explanation?" Andrew inquired.

"Of course, but only to rub it in," Mary said.

"What do you mean?" Andrew asked.

"Instead of saying it to help me look at the positive side of the situation, it was his response when I asked him if he thought John would still speak to me," Mary explained.

Andrew chuckled and nodded. "And what did your mother say when she found out what she'd done?" he asked.

"I never told her," Mary responded. "Neither did Dad."

"Why? " Andrew inquired.

"Because we both knew it would break her heart to think she may have done something to upset one of her children," Mary said.

"Even Mary," James quipped.

Everyone laughed quietly at James' wisecrack.

Mary glared at James and a devious smile developed on her face. "As I recall, you were the one who was always making Mom feel guilty."

"What do you mean?" James asked innocently.

"I seem to remember a goldfish that died because someone forgot to feed it," Mary said.

"Oh, that," James said.

"I didn't hear about that one," Elizabeth said.

"It was nothing," James assured.

"Mary?" Elizabeth asked.

Mary giggled over her victory. "James didn't want to be blamed for killing the fish. He knew that it was his responsibility and if he killed it, there would be no more pets. So he looked for a way that he could place the blame on his little sister. It had been so long since he had fed the poor fish that he had a hard time even finding its food. He finally located it in the cupboard next to the Ajax."

"I'm sure no one wants to hear this Mary," James said hopefully.

"Yes we do," everyone said in unison.

"Thank you," Mary responded. "Anyway, he knew that it was my job to clean the sinks, so figured I was the last one to use the cleanser. He mixed a little with the fish food, then preceded to feed his dead fish."

"This is embarrassing," James said. His face was becoming uncomfortably warm and he was glad everyone's eyes were fixed on Mary.

Mary continued. "Of course, the water turned blue

and James squeezed out a few fake tears and went crying to mother. She rushed to his side and asked what had happened. He took her to the fish bowel and showed her the floating carcass. He proceeded to tell her the lid wasn't on the fish food when he got it out and that I must have spilled Ajax in the container when I cleaned the basin."

"A logical conclusion," James said defensively.

"I suppose," Mary said, "but the plan backfired when Mom confessed that she was the last one to use the cleanser. She was so upset, she started crying with him. Only her tears were real."

"So were mine after I realized my plan had failed," James confessed. He pulled a pen from his front pocket and motioned for Elizabeth to hand him the notebook on top of the piano. "I think it's time to change the subject before Mary destroys everyone's image of me."

"I'm sure we'd all love to hear more, but James is right," Anna said. "We'd better take a minute to discuss the funeral before it gets too late to call Mr. Watkins."

"I'll call and arrange for the church," Mary volunteered. "I assume we'll be looking at Thursday for the funeral?"

"Mr. Price seemed to think that would be fine," James confirmed.

Elizabeth began taking notes.

"I think maybe we should ask Sarah to give a short eulogy," Rachel suggested.

"We can ask her, but I don't think she's capable of giving a short anythi—ouch!" Andrew protested as Rachel jabbed him in the ribs with her elbow.

"He is right," James said with a chuckle.

"Perhaps you could help her write it," Anna suggested to Rachel.

"That's a good idea," Rachel agreed. "I'll do that."

"I guess the only thing left is a speaker and the music," James said. "I suppose I should say something as the oldest and Anna, I believe the music should be your department."

"Certainly," Anna responded. Everyone watched in silence as she stood and walked across the room to the bookshelf and pulled down a hymnal. "I know just the songs." Her eyes clouded as she began thumbing through the index. "I think this will be the closing song. It was Mom's favorite."

Anna stood motionless in the center of the room as she stared at the open hymnbook.

"Are you okay?" Rachel asked.

As if oblivious to Rachel's question, Anna lifted her eyes from the open page. "Let's sing it for her now," she said.

A feeling of warmth seemed to envelop everyone in response to Anna's request. No one spoke, but James and Elizabeth moved from the piano bench. Elizabeth sat where Anna had been and James positioned himself on the arm of the sofa.

Anna sat at the upright mahogany piano and began to play. The rich tone of the instrument filled the room and everyone began to sing. Anna and Rachel blended their soprano voices while Mary and Elizabeth sang alto. John and Andrew shared the tenor notes and James was the lone bass. Tears flowed freely as one by one, each of the women were overcome by the almost tangible feeling in the room and their voices waned.

When she could no longer see the notes, Anna rested her slender fingers on the soundless keyboard. Silent tears were shed leaving only the melancholy resonance of a male trio singing the final words of the chorus: "God be with you 'till we meet again."

CHAPTER ELEVEN

"I'll go try Mr. Watkins." James stood and moved towards the kitchen, but stopped. "Was that the door?"

"I didn't hear anything," Elizabeth said.

James walked to the front door and opened it. "Guess you were right," he said when he didn't see anyone. He started to close the door.

"Hey," a voice said from outside.

James opened the door again and popped his head around the corner. He stepped out onto the porch, pulling the door closed behind him. "I wondered if you were going to sit in your car all afternoon."

"Yeah...well, I heard the singing," Thomas said. His hair was combed and his clothes tidy.

It wasn't clear to James what the singing had to do with Thomas's decision to come to the house, but he saw no reason to question it. "Let's go inside where it's warm," he suggested.

Thomas looked apprehensive. "I don't know if that's a good idea."

"You've come this far," James reminded him.

Thomas nodded.

James opened the door and stepped inside. Thomas followed sheepishly behind.

As they stepped inside the front room, Anna gasped. "Thomas!" she screamed and jumped up from the piano bench. She ran to Thomas and wrapped her arms around his neck. "We're so glad you're here," she said softly in his ear.

Thomas stood quietly without returning the embrace.

Anna released her hold and stood next to Thomas with her right arm around his waist.

"It's good to see you Thomas," Elizabeth said sincerely as she took his coat.

"Yeah, Thomas," Rachel echoed, "it's good to see you."

Andrew smiled and nodded an informal greeting.

"Hey guy, how you doin'?" John asked.

Mary sat in silence as the tension in the room increased. She fidgeted uncomfortably in her seat as everyone's eyes slowly turned in her direction. "We need to be going," she said to John and stood up. "I'll go get Cody and Samuel."

"Don't you think you should say something to your brother, Mary?" John asked.

"I'll go get the boys," Mary returned sternly. As she left the room to go find her children, she hollered over her shoulder, "I'll get our coats and meet you at the car, John,"

"What about Mr. Watkins?" James called after her.

"You can call me later and tell me what you found out," Mary yelled back.

John stood up and walked toward the door leading to the kitchen. He stopped and turned so he was facing the others. "I'm sorry Thomas . . . everybody," he apologized. "It's been hard—she's really struggling. I'm sorry." He left the room in obvious frustration and embarrassment.

James looked at Thomas as though he wanted to say something.

"It's okay," Thomas said. "Maybe I'd better just go."

"There's no need for that," James assured.

"I guess I should have expected it," Thomas said.

Mary's performance left everyone unsure of how to best respond. Anna finally broke the silence. "Why don't you sit down?" she asked Thomas and pointed at the rocking chair.

Thomas walked to the chair and sat down. Anna returned to the piano bench and James took Mary's seat on the sofa, next to Elizabeth.

An eerie silence invaded the room. Thomas had no desire to talk about himself, so determined it safest to direct any conversation that ensued. "Who's Mr. Watkins?" he asked.

"We're not sure," Rachel responded.

Thomas looked puzzled.

"His business card was found in Mom's purse," James clarified. "I was just about to go call him and see if he could tell us why she had his card."

"What does he do?" Thomas inquired, obviously struggling to keep the conversation going.

"He's a salesman," Anna said. She reached behind her and took the envelope with the contents of her mother's purse. She pulled out the card and handed it to Thomas.

"So what are we waiting for?" he asked James. "Let's go call him." Thomas stood up and motioned for James to follow.

James smiled as he stood and walked over to

Thomas. He took the business card from Thomas' hand. "I guess we'll be back," he said to the others as he led Thomas into the kitchen.

James sat down in front of the small desk supporting the telephone and Thomas sat at the kitchen table.

"Don't you want to be in with the others?" James asked curiously.

Thomas shook his head.

"Okay," James said, "but it's usually pretty boring listening to one side of a telephone conversation."

Thomas just shrugged.

James picked up the telephone receiver and carefully dialed the numbers printed on the front of the card. He could feel the nerves in his stomach spring into action as the connection was made and the ringing started. After five rings, an answering machine picked-up: This is Joseph Watkins, I'm . . ."

"Hello," a deep and breathless male voice said over the top of the continuing message. "Sorry. Hang on, let me shut that thing off."

James could hear some fumbling in the background, then the recorded voice stopped.

"Hello," Joseph said.

"Mr. Watkins?" James asked.

"Yes. Look, I'm sorry about the machine. I just walked through the door," Joseph explained.

"Don't worry about it," James said.

"So what can I do for you?" Joseph asked.

"My name is James Cooper and I was calling about my mother," James said.

"Uh . . . your mother?" Joseph asked. "I'm afraid

you've got me at a disadvantage. I don't recall a . . . Mrs. Cooper, was it?"

"Yes, Martha," James said.

"Oh! Martha," Joseph repeated with enthusiasm. "Yes, I met her on the plane to Atlanta over the weekend. I thought she was on a cruise."

"That was the plan," James confirmed. "But I'm afraid there have been some problems."

"What kind of problems?" Joseph asked.

"Well, actually Mr. Watkins, I'm afraid my mother is dead," James said.

"Oh my," Joseph whispered. "What happened?"

"It appears she somehow ended up in a bad part of San Juan where she was the victim of a robbery followed by a fatal gunshot wound. That's really all we know," James replied.

"I'm so sorry," Joseph said. "This must be awful for your family."

"It's difficult," James said, "but we're doing okay."

"I'm so glad you called, but how did you get my name?" Joseph asked.

"Your business card. It was among the contents of Mom's purse," James explained.

"Yes, of course," Joseph said. "I gave it to her when we landed here in Atlanta."

"I see," James said in disappointment. "We were kind of hoping you could tell us something about Mother or the trip that might shed some light on what happened."

"I wish I could help you, but my entire knowledge of her comes from a few hours on a plane and a few minutes at the airport," Joseph said apologetically.

"No, that's all right," James said.

"If it's any help," Joseph added, "I think your mother was a wonderful person. I really felt close to her after our visit. The way she talked about her family, I could tell she was a special woman. That's why I gave her my business card. I hoped to keep in touch."

"Thank you, Mr. Watkins. She was very special," James agreed. "And it does help to hear you say that."

"Please, call me Joseph."

"Okay, Joseph," James said. "I won't keep you any longer, but thanks again. You were probably one of the last people to really talk with Mom before she died. The fact that she kept your business card tells me she must have thought you were pretty special too."

"It's my pleasure," Joseph said. "It was an honor to meet her."

Though he knew there was little more to say, James could not bring himself to terminate the conversation. "I'm glad you feel that way," he said. "Listen, maybe we could talk again later when you have some free time?"

"Sure," Joseph agreed. "I'll be here all weekend. Call anytime."

"I wouldn't want to interrupt your Christmas plans," James said.

"Oh, don't worry about that, I don't have any plans."

"No plans for Christmas?" James asked. "What about your family?"

"Well, I'm not married," Joseph explained.

"What about your parents or brothers and sisters?"

"I'm an only child," Joseph responded, "and my parents are in New Zealand for the holidays."

Thomas tapped James on the knee. "Are you thinking what I think you're thinking?" he whispered.

James nodded. "Look, Joseph, I know this is kind of a strange suggestion, but why don't you come spend Christmas with our family."

"I couldn't do that," Joseph responded.

"You'd be doing us a favor," James suggested. "We could hear about the time you spent with Mother and you could have a real Christmas. Everyone wins."

Joseph didn't say anything.

"So what do you say?" James asked.

"I don't know . . ." Joseph said.

"Joseph, think of it as a Christmas gift for our mother."

Joseph sighed. "I don't usually do things like this," he said, "but your mother did make quite an impression on me. I don't know what it was about her, but . . ."

"Then you'll come?" Joseph interrupted.

"Well, believe it or not, I was actually coming your way for business on Tuesday. I suppose I could try to get an earlier flight—if you're sure about this."

"I'm sure," James exclaimed. "Everyone will be excited about having you with us."

"Why don't you give me your number and I'll call my travel agent right now and then call you back," Joseph offered.

James gave Joseph the requested information and hung up the phone. "He may be coming here," he said to Thomas.

"So I gathered," Thomas said. "I'm glad he's coming."

"Me too," James confessed. "It felt good to talk to him about Mom." James looked at Thomas then added, "And no one should spend Christmas alone."

"Yeah," Thomas agreed as he stared at the floor. "And I guess talking to Mr. Watkins is probably the only way I'll be able to get close to Mom now."

James smiled and nodded as he considered Thomas' statement.

After several minutes of somewhat trivial conversation, the telephone rang. James quickly reached for the receiver and picked it up. "Hello."

"Hello, James, this is Joseph."

"So what did you find out?" James asked.

"Would you believe the soonest flight I could get was for Sunday afternoon?" Joseph said.

"That's great, then you'll be here in time for our annual Christmas Eve dinner." James replied.

"Okay, great," Joseph said, "but there is one small problem. I was able to get a hotel room, but there are no rental cars available any earlier than the one I already have reserved for Tuesday morning."

"That's no problem, I'll pick you up. And forget the hotel room, you can stay here," James offered.

"I already feel bad enough that I'm interrupting your Christmas Eve festivities to pick me up, but to expect you to put me up is asking too much," Joseph suggested.

"Nonsense," James said. "It's the least we can do. We'd love to have you."

"Well, if you're sure it's not an imposition," Joseph said.

"Not at all," James confirmed.

"My flight arrives at 3:42 p.m. Sunday."

"Great. There will be plenty of time to get there after church," James said. "How will I know you?"

"Um, let's see," Joseph said as he thought, "I'll wear my Christmas baseball cap. It's red, with a green brim and a picture of Santa imprinted on the front."

"Okay, see you Sunday" James said. He put the telephone down and smiled at Thomas. "I guess you heard."

Thomas nodded.

"Let's tell the others," James said as he stood up. He waited for Thomas to stand, then walked to the front room where the others were still sitting in their same places and visiting quietly.

"Well?" Anna asked anxiously.

"He's coming here for Christmas," James announced. "I'll pick him up at the airport after church on Sunday."

"How did you manage that?" Rachel queried.

"He has no family around and was planning to be in town on Tuesday anyway, so I invited him to join us for Christmas," James answered.

"Why was he coming here on Tuesday?" Andrew asked.

"He said he had business here. A sales call I suspect," James replied.

"So where did he meet Mom?" Rachel asked.

"On the flight to Atlanta. He was quite taken by her and said he would be happy to talk to us," James replied.

"What else did he say?" Anna asked.

"Nothing really," James responded. "But he seemed like a very nice man and there was something about the way he spoke of Mother. I'm sure you'll all feel it when you meet him."

James returned to his seat next to Elizabeth.

Thomas remained standing, but didn't speak. His hand was leaning on the back of the rocking chair where he had been seated earlier.

"Why don't you sit down, Thomas?" Andrew asked.

Thomas walked to the front of the chair and seated himself. Grateful that he was not the topic of conversation, but still somewhat uncomfortable, he nervously chewed on his lower lip while the others continued questioning James.

"Where will Mr. Watkins be staying?" Elizabeth asked. She looked at Rachel and winked.

James' eyes grew wide and Thomas chuckled.

"I hope you don't mind, but I said he could stay here?" James confessed.

"Typical man," Elizabeth jested. "Commit my services, then get my permission."

"I'm sorry," James apologized. "I was just so excited. Is it okay?"

"And if it's not?" Elizabeth asked. She was unable to maintain a straight face and began to laugh. "You know it's fine," she said. "So what time do you pick him up?"

"He gets in a little before four, so I'll go straight from church," James said.

Anna sat forward in her seat. "Kind of eerie, don't you think?"

"What do you mean?" James asked.

"Isn't that when Mom was supposed to come home?" Anna queried.

"I think you're right, Anna," Elizabeth said.

"Actually, I think it's rather appropriate," James suggested. "Mom seemed to think a lot of Joseph and he was one of the last people to see her. It's only right that he represent her on the return trip she wasn't able to make."

"So what does he look like?" Rachel asked.

"Who?" James asked.

"Mr. Watkins," Rachel said.

James shook his head.

"You know, Joseph," Rachel clarified.

"I know who Mr. Watkins is, but how should I know what he looks like," James responded condescendingly. "And what difference does it make?"

Andrew sat forward, turned and looked up at Rachel. "Yeah," he protested, "why should you care what he looks like?"

"I don't care, but how else will James know who to pick up?" Rachel reasoned.

James laughed and nodded in understanding. "He'll be wearing a Christmas baseball cap."

"Thank you," Rachel said smugly.

"Well, now that that's settled, we'd better be going," Andrew suggested as he reached backward over his shoulders and grabbed Rachel's hands.

"Yeah, I'd better go too," Anna said.

"Why don't you all come to church with us on Sunday?" James suggested.

"That's a good idea," Elizabeth agreed. "Then we'll all be here when James gets back with Joseph."

"And it should give us time to visit with Mr. Watkins before we get too involved with final meal preparations." Anna suggested.

"Can I still sleep in?" Andrew asked.

Rachel shook her head and rolled her eyes. "We'll be there," she confirmed.

"Great, I'll call Mary and let her know what we're doing," James said.

After Elizabeth brought everyone's coats to the room, Anna and Rachel stood and Rachel helped Andrew to his feet. The sisters both looked at Thomas, then at each other and walked past him without speaking. James and Elizabeth escorted them to the door. Thomas remained seated with his back to them.

"Will we see you Sunday, Thomas?" Anna asked before leaving.

"I'll see," Thomas responded.

"We love you," she said, as she stepped outside. "Welcome home."

When the others had gone, Elizabeth excused herself to go check on the children. Thomas sat rocking in the wooden chair and James stood in front of him.

"Why don't you come with us Sunday?" James asked. "Then you can go to the airport with me."

"I don't know, maybe," Thomas replied. He stood and walked toward the front door.

"Will you stay for dinner?" James offered.

"No, I need to go," Thomas said.

"I hope you didn't let Mary get to you," James said.

"I'm used to it," Thomas responded.

"She'll come around," James assured. "It'll just take a little time."

"Yeah," Thomas acknowledged, "and there's always tomorrow, right?"

CHAPTER TWELVE

Mary and John, along with their boys were the first to meet James, Elizabeth and their children at the church. Anna arrived with Rachel and Andrew a short time later. In spite of the crisp chill in the wintry morning air, everyone stayed outside to visit. The peace they found in each other's company provided more warmth than the bright sun reflecting from the snow covered grass and treetops.

As the time to go inside neared, Mary began to grow restless. "I knew he wouldn't come," she said to the others.

"Do you blame him?" John asked.

"Look, let's just go inside," Anna suggested. She took five-year-old Jessica by the hand and looked at Elizabeth who nodded her approval.

Anna and Jessica began their ascent up the front steps of the church. Elizabeth and Lisa followed behind.

"Come on, let's go," James said to Allen. He put his arm around his son's shoulders and together they rushed to catch up with Elizabeth and Lisa who were just stepping inside the front doors.

Rachel and Andrew looked at Mary and John.

"Why don't you take the boys inside," Mary said to John. "I'll be in shortly."

She gently nudged each of her boys toward their father.

"I'll save you a spot," John said as he picked up two-year-old Samuel.

"Here," Rachel said to Cody, "why don't you take Uncle Andrew's hand."

Andrew extended his right hand and wrapped his gloved fingers around Cody's. He then offered his left arm to Rachel, who graciously accepted and linked her arm with his. The three of them followed John and Samuel into the church.

With the others inside, Mary turned and walked back to the parking lot. She took her keys from her purse and opened the driver's side door of their car. Tossing her purse on the seat, she climbed behind the steering wheel and placed the key into the ignition. She hesitated, then put her face into her hands and began to cry. Her mournful weeping soon turned to uncontrolled sobbing.

"Why, Mother?" she sobbed aloud as if Martha was in the seat next to her. "Why did you have to leave us now? Couldn't you have at least waited until things were right between you and Thomas? The day he left, I promised myself I wouldn't speak to him until you told me it was all right. Now with you gone, I've lost him too. How can I forgive him after the way he treated you? Why should he forgive me after the way I've treated him? Oh mother, we still need you. How will our family ever come back together without you?"

Mary sat in the car and cried until there were no tears left to shed. Though she felt better for having expressed her feelings, she still hurt inside because of her losses. Trapped between pride and compassion, she could see no way to resolve her conflict.

Taking a tissue from her purse, Mary wiped her eyes. She used the rearview mirror to adjust her makeup, then got out of the car and went inside. She was completely unaware that the occupant of a car parked across the street had been watching her.

When Mary took her seat next to John, he could see that she'd been crying. "Are you okay?" he whispered.

"I'm fine," she whispered back. She laid her head on his shoulder and listened to the words being offered from the pulpit.

Everyone seemed to notice the unusual reverence that persisted throughout the meeting. It was so real that there was no need to discuss it. Each member of the family could sense that the others felt the same thing. Even the children sat more attentively than usual. Somehow, hearing the story of the first Christmas transcended everyone's pain. Perhaps the comfort came from their faith in He who came of a miraculous birth and would one day overcome death.

At the conclusion of the service, a small group of people wishing to offer their sympathy to James and his family gathered at the end of the pew and blocked the passage into the aisle.

Concerned that he might not make it to the airport on time, James devised a plan for a quick escape. "I'll sneak out the other way," he said to Elizabeth. "See you at home."

James squeezed passed the people behind him and exited into the aisle at the other end of the bench where they had been seated. Moving rapidly to the back of the chapel, he made his way to a side door. He hurried through the snow across the lawn to the parking lot and his car.

"Does the offer still stand?"

James turned around to see Thomas leaning against a neighboring car. His hair had been cut and he was dressed in a neatly pressed suit. "Of course it does, get in," James said.

James unlocked the doors and the brothers climbed into the front seat.

"Why didn't you come in?" James asked as he backed out of the parking space and pulled onto the street.

"I did," Thomas replied.

"I didn't see you."

"I know, I sat in the back," Thomas explained.

"Why didn't you come sit with the rest of the family?" James asked.

"I came in late."

"Is that the only reason?" James asked

"You know it's not," Thomas said.

James didn't respond.

They drove through the main part of town and onto the freeway before either of them spoke again.

"I'm ready to come back," Thomas announced.

"And we're happy to have you," James assured.

"You know that letter from Mom you brought to me?"

"Yes," James answered.

"She said it's not too late even though she's dead. Do you believe that?" Thomas asked sincerely.

"It doesn't matter what I believe, Thomas. The question is do you believe it?"

"I want to," Thomas confessed, "but I'm not sure that I can."

"What's so hard about believing that your mother's love exists beyond the grave?" James asked.

"But how can it? She's not here to give it?" Thomas reasoned.

"Thomas, love knows no bounds. Do you think Mom felt Dad's love any less when he was in Korea?"

"No, but they could write letters to each other," Thomas argued.

"And Mom wrote a letter to you," James said. "Love isn't something you hear or see, it's something you feel inside. Do you know what I mean?"

"I believe I do," Thomas said as he reached into his jacket pocket and pulled out an envelope.

"What's that?" James asked.

"A letter I wrote to Mom in response to her letter to me."

"You can still feel her love, can't you? Just like you feel Dad's love," James suggested. "And you can feel your brother's and sisters' love too."

Thomas sat silently as he stared at the road ahead.

"You can even feel Mary's love, can't you Thomas?" James asked after a few moments of silence.

"That's what confuses me, James. Deep inside I can feel it, but then it gets run over by what I see her do and don't hear her say."

"I know," James acknowledged, "but you have to get beyond that, sometimes even ignore it so you can concentrate on what you feel inside."

"But it's sure nice to see, hear, and feel it," Thomas

said. "And I know that may still be possible with Mary; but not with Mom."

"Oh, I don't know," James disputed. "Mom's influence will be around for a while. I think you'll see and hear plenty of things that express her love for you."

Thomas nodded in agreement. "And I guess there are still things I can do to express my love for her," he said.

"Exactly," James confirmed. "The way you choose to live your life is an expression of your love for both Mom and Dad. The more you live like they would have you live . . . well, you know."

"Yeah," Thomas said. He cleared his throat and took in a deep breath. "James, I got a job yesterday."

A broad smile brightened James face. He reached across the seat and gently slapped Thomas on the thigh. "Congratulations," he said. "Was it one of those construction jobs you told me about?"

"Nope," Thomas said. "Actually it's for Mr. Lyn."

"Anna's boss?" James asked.

"Don't act so surprised," Thomas kidded.

"How did that come about?"

"Anna slipped a note into my pocket when I was at your house on Friday. I guess she put it in there when she was hugging me or something," Thomas explained. "Anyway, I called her yesterday and she said Mr. Lyn has been talking about wanting an apprentice so he could turn his business over to someone he trusted when he retires."

"He must have been pretty impressed by you," James suggested.

"Well, I hope I had something to do with it," Thomas said.

"So when do you start?" James asked.

"After Mom's funeral," Thomas answered.

"Speaking of the funeral," James interjected, "I was wondering if you'd like to take an active part?"

"I've been thinking about that, and I believe I'd like to," Thomas said.

"What would you like to do?" James asked.

"You know that song you were all singing at your house?"

"Yes, 'God Be With You,'" James said.

"Maybe I could sing that," Thomas offered.

A cold chill moved down James' spine and spread throughout his entire body as he relived the feeling at their father's funeral when Thomas sang the closing number. His powerful baritone voice impacted everyone in attendance. Thomas could barely finish the number for the tears and vowed never to sing in public again.

"That would be wonderful," James said. "Mom would like that."

The remaining few miles to the airport passed in silence.

Last-minute holiday travelers meant heavy traffic at the airport. James skillfully maneuvered through the sea of vehicles to the parking lot nearest the terminal entrance. After parking the car he and Thomas rushed inside to meet Joseph.

"It's a lot bigger than I remember," Thomas observed upon entering the terminal.

"You haven't been here in a while," James noted.

"Not since I was a kid," Thomas said.

"Unfortunately, I come here more than I care to," James lamented.

Thomas followed James past the large Christmas display to the video monitors listing flight information. They found the appropriate flight and made their way to the specified gate.

The wide corridor leading to the gate ended in a large open area shared by four terminal gates. The number of other people apparently waiting to greet arriving passengers amazed Thomas. All the chairs were occupied and everyone who was left standing had little personal space. Thomas felt claustrophobic. "Is it always this crowded?" he asked.

"It must be the holiday," James answered. "Just stick close to me so we don't get separated."

James forced his way through the crowd until he could see the door labeled E9. Thomas was close behind.

The sign above the entrance was flashing *ARRIVED* and a young woman in a blue uniform with gold trim opened the beige steel door. Passengers could be seen ascending the tube-like passage leading from the airplane.

James strained his eyes to look for a man in a red and green baseball cap. If he stood on tiptoes, he was tall enough to see over most of the people in front of him.

Thomas was built more like his father and had no difficulty peering over the crowd. As more passengers filed by, he became increasingly anxious. "I guess these must be the people from first class," Thomas said.

"Yep," James agreed, "but the rest will be coming soon."

After a brief disruption in the flow, another steady stream of people emerged.

"Is that him?" Thomas asked, pointing at a man wearing a baseball cap.

"He looks younger than I imagined, but he's the only one with a hat," James said as he pushed through the rows of people standing in front of him. He approached the man who appeared to be about his own age and extended his right hand. "Joseph Watkins?"

"That's right," Joseph said. He had a travel bag over his shoulder and a briefcase in his right hand. A folded newspaper was tucked neatly under his left arm. He switched the briefcase to his left hand and greeted James with a handshake. "You must be James," he said.

James smiled and nodded. "Here, let me carry that." He took Joseph's briefcase in his left hand. "Let's move to where there's some breathing room," James suggested.

"Good idea," Joseph agreed. He followed James out to the corridor and into an area with a little more elbow-room.

James extended his right arm. "This is my brother Thoma—" He paused when he realized Thomas was not there. "I'm sorry, I thought he was right behind us."

Joseph smiled. "That's fine," he said.

James turned back toward the crowd and began looking for his brother. He spotted Thomas still looking down the jetway. "Thomas!" James yelled and waved his arm.

Thomas turned his head and nodded at James. He worked his way through the crowd and slowly walked to where James and Joseph were standing.

"I thought you were right behind us," James said.

Thomas didn't say anything.

"Joseph, this is my brother Thomas," James said.

"Pleased to meet you, Thomas," Joseph said and extended his open hand.

Thomas grasped Joseph's hand firmly, smiled and nodded.

"Do we need to go to Baggage Claim?" James inquired.

"Nope," Joseph responded, "I've learned to be a light traveler."

"Great," Joseph said. "Let's head to the car."

"I need to make one phone call if that's all right," Joseph said.

"Sure," James responded. "There's a telephone over there." He pointed to a bank of payphones on the wall.

James and Thomas waited while Joseph went to place his call.

"Are you okay?" James asked Thomas.

"Can't you feel it?" Thomas asked.

"Feel what?" James asked in return

"That strange feeling."

"Strange how?" James asked. "Like we shouldn't be here?"

"No," Thomas replied. "It's . . . it's like we should be here?"

James looked confused. "We are here, Thomas."

"I know," Thomas acknowledged. "Maybe that's why

it seems strange." He started walking away from James. "I'll be over here when you're ready to go," he said, pointing to some plants near the end of the corridor.

"Okay," James said, still feeling somewhat perplexed by Thomas' behavior. He walked over to the telephones where Joseph was just finishing his call.

"Sorry to keep you," Joseph apologized. "I'd forgotten to cancel my reservation at the hotel. I figured I'd better take care of it as soon as I could."

James nodded in understanding. "Well, should we go?" he asked.

Joseph picked up his bag and placed the strap over his shoulder. "Are you sure you don't want me to carry that briefcase?" he asked James.

"No, I'm fine," James assured.

"Where's Thomas?" Joseph asked.

"He's over . . ." James started laughing. "I seem to keep losing him. He was right over there by those plants."

Joseph looked around and started chuckling. "There he is," Joseph said pointing toward the gate.

Thomas was standing amongst the crowd watching as the remaining passengers exited the plane and entered the terminal corridor.

CHAPTER THIRTEEN

"Everyone," James said as he entered the front room with Joseph, "this is Joseph Watkins." He placed Joseph's bags next to the door.

A light snow had started to fall outside, so both men dusted off their shoulders.

Joseph took off his hat as he smiled and nodded. "This looks like quite a group," he observed.

"It's a pleasure to meet you," Elizabeth said. "I'm James' wife, Elizabeth."

"Nice meeting you," Joseph responded.

"This is Mary," John said as he extended his hand. "And I'm John."

Joseph shook John's hand and acknowledged Mary with a wave. "It's a pleasure," he said.

"Hi," Rachel offered, "I'm Rachel and this is my husband Andrew."

Andrew stood and shook Joseph's hand, then returned to his seat without speaking.

"Hello Mr. Watkins, I'm Anna."

Joseph stared at Anna briefly before responding, "Hello Anna. And please, call me Joseph."

Anna acknowledged Joseph's request with a soft smile.

"James, why don't you show Joseph to his room so he can freshen up before we get started," Elizabeth suggested.

"Right," James said. He picked up Joseph's briefcase and travel bag. "Joseph, you can just follow me."

Joseph walked with James into the kitchen and down the hallway.

James returned to the front room. "Everyone else should be here soon," he said.

"Who else are we expecting?" Elizabeth asked in surprise.

"Thomas met me at the church and rode to the airport with me," James explained. "We dropped him off so he could pick up his car. He'll be here shortly with our other guest."

"Our other guest?" Elizabeth queried.

James smiled. "Thomas bumped into an old acquaintance."

"Oh, this should be good," Mary complained.

John glared at Mary from across the room.

"It's okay Mary, really," James assured.

"I can hardly wait," Mary said sarcastically.

A car could be heard pulling into the driveway. James looked out the window. "They're here," he announced.

Joseph entered the front room from the kitchen just as Thomas opened the front door and stood in the opening. Thomas' face was beaming with excitement.

"Did you tell them?" Thomas breathlessly asked James.

"I told them you bumped into an old acquaintance at the airport," James responded.

"Oh," Thomas said, still trying to catch his breath. "Well, she's right behind me."

"She?" Mary asked. "My, he's actually taking interest in a woman. Of course, she probably didn't need his help."

"Mary!" John said.

"It's okay, John," Thomas assured. He turned and looked at Mary.

Mary lowered her eyes to the ground.

"Mary, I know you're upset about the way I treated Mom after Dad died," Thomas said. "But things will be different now, I promise."

Mary didn't acknowledge Thomas' assurance.

"It's all right, Mary," a soft voice said from behind Thomas.

Mary lifted her head and joined the others who were now staring in Thomas' direction.

"It's all right," Martha repeated as she stepped from behind Thomas. "Things will be different now. And by the way, Merry Christmas."

Anna gasped and put her hand over her mouth. Rachel started crying and Elizabeth sat quietly, shaking her head.

Mary jumped to her feet. "How?" she asked as she ran across the room. Anna and Rachel followed closely behind.

Mary stood in front of Thomas and her mother with her arms outstretched. "I don't know whom to hug first," she said through her tears.

Martha chuckled. "Take him," she said as she extended her open arms to Rachel and Anna.

Mary wrapped her arms around Thomas' neck. "I'm so sorry," she whispered into his ear. "I had no right to treat you that way. I hope you can forgive me."

"I'm sorry too," Thomas offered. "And of course I forgive you, but only if you do the same for me."

Mary let go of her brother and squeezed in between Rachel and Anna. "God knew we still needed you," she said as she wrapped her arms around Martha.

"I'll wait until your sisters have spoken with her," Elizabeth whispered to James between sniffles.

"Come on," James said. Putting his arm around Elizabeth's waist, he escorted her to where they could join the joyful reunion. He looked over his shoulder at John and Andrew who were still sitting. "Well get up here," he said, "you don't need permission."

John and Andrew enthusiastically joined the others.

Joseph watched in amazement as Martha's family embraced her and everyone shed quiet tears of joy.

"Are you okay, Joseph?" Anna asked when she noticed the wonder in his gaze.

"I've never seen anything like this," Joseph said as he wiped his eyes. "I don't have any brothers or sisters. You guys really love each other, don't you?"

"We sure do," Anna confirmed.

"Why don't we all sit down and let Mom tell us about her adventure?" James suggested. He stepped into the kitchen and returned with some chairs. He placed them next to the sofa so they faced the rocking chair. "Thomas, John and Joseph, why don't you sit over there?" he said as he pointed to the chairs from the kitchen. He then took his seat on the piano bench next to Elizabeth.

Mary, Rachel, and Anna sat on the sofa and Andrew

took his usual spot on the floor in front of his wife.

Martha sat in the rocking chair. As she looked at her children and Joseph, she grinned and shook her head. "I feel like I'm on trial," she said.

"Just center stage," Anna corrected. "We're anxious to hear what happened."

"I can only tell you my side of the story," Martha apologized.

"That's okay," John said.

"Well, like I told the boys on the way home," Martha began, "things went fine until I got to San Juan." She looked at Joseph and smiled. "Joseph was a great help. He listened to me brag about my family all the way to Atlanta. Then he helped me get to my next flight."

"Is that when you gave her your card?" Anna asked Joseph.

"Yep," Joseph said. "I was hoping she would keep in touch and add some spice to my boring life."

Everyone laughed at Joseph's comment.

"Well, I was glad you gave me the card and I put it in my purse. I almost lost it, but a nice young man named James, I mean Jim, saw me drop it and returned it to me," Martha explained.

"Enough about the card," Mary protested.

"I'm sorry," Martha said, "but I thought it was important to mention, especially since Joseph is here as our guest." Martha looked at Joseph and winked. "Anyway, I got to Puerto Rico and even got my bags to the shuttle. I had time for something to eat, so I bought me a hotdog."

"With extra mustard, no doubt," Elizabeth said.

"Of course," Martha acknowledged. "And that's what got me into trouble."

"I told you all that mustard wasn't good for you," James jested.

Martha rolled her eyes and continued. "I spilled mustard on my blouse and went into a restroom to clean it off. I guess I took longer than I thought and missed the shuttle."

"That must have been awful," Rachel sympathized.

"It was," Martha confirmed. "I don't know when I've been so scared." She hesitated. "Actually, I do, but we'll come to that in a minute."

"Anyway . . ." Mary prodded.

"I had someone at the airport call the Cruise Company. They said I'd have to take a taxi, but after watching some of the taxis at the airport and remembering what Sarah said about it being unsafe for a woman to ride alone in one, I decided that wasn't a good option."

"So what did you do?" Anna asked.

"I ignored my own advice to you children. I let fear and logic override the feeling deep inside and accepted help from a stranger."

"Why would you do that?" Mary asked.

"She said she could get me to the pier on time if I took a guagua. Jim, the young man who returned Joseph's business card, told me he was taking a guagua to the beach, so I figured it must be safe."

"What's a gwa-gwa?" John asked.

"It's basically a van crammed with people," Martha answered. "Sort of a private bus, I guess."

"So then what?" Elizabeth asked.

"I went with the woman on the guagua and we stopped a few blocks from the pier. She said we had to walk the rest of the way." Martha shuddered. "Like a fool, I followed her into a dark alley where she demanded my purse."

"What did you do?" Anna asked.

"I froze. I was so scared, I couldn't move. But then she threw me to the ground and pulled a gun from under her shirt. When she fired the gun in the air I knew she meant business, so I gave her my purse," Martha explained.

"I'm confused," Andrew said. "How did you get on the ship if your purse had been stolen?"

"In spite of her rambling, Sarah, bless her heart, gave me some more good advice and fortunately I listened," Martha responded. "She told me not to keep my money or my credit card in my purse, so when we landed in Puerto Rico, I put my tickets, travelers checks and credit card in my stocking. I kept some loose change plus a five and a ten-dollar bill in my handbag, just enough to get something to eat and to cover any emergencies. It's just as well since I had to pay for the guagua."

"So who was found dead?" Mary asked.

"Oh, that reminds me," James interrupted, "I'd better go call Chief Rosen and let him know they're planning on sending the wrong woman from Puerto Rico." He got up and went into the kitchen.

"I don't know," Martha said in response to Mary's question. "After I gave her my purse, the lady ran off down the street. I could see the ship from where I was, so I walked to the port and got there just in time. I was a bit shaken, but I was safe. That's all I know."

"It's likely the dead woman was the one who stole your purse," Joseph said.

"I suppose you're right," Martha agreed. "I feel bad for her. If I hadn't been so scared by the gun, I would have shown her that there was no money in the purse. Then maybe she wouldn't have gotten killed for it."

Everyone sat quietly as they contemplated the reality of Martha's last comment.

"We can't tell you how grateful we are that you're safe," Mary said to Martha, "but can we change the subject?"

"Maybe you could tell us about your cruise," Rachel suggested.

"There will be plenty of time to talk about that later," Martha said. "Why don't you tell me what's new around here since my . . . 'death'?"

"Nothing much," Anna said.

Andrew laid his head back on Rachel's lap. He looked at her with a questioning twinkle in his eye. Rachel nodded her approval.

"We're having a baby," Andrew calmly said.

Anna screamed and wrapped her arms around Rachel's neck.

"Oh, that's wonderful. Congratulations," Martha said. "How far along are you?"

"Just five weeks," Rachel responded.

"The fun is just beginning," Mary said. She reached over and patted Rachel's tummy.

"What's going on?" James asked as he walked back into the room.

"Rachel's pregnant!" Elizabeth said.

"Well congratulations," James said. "That's even more exciting than Thomas' news."

"What news?" Martha asked.

"Anna got me a job at the store," Thomas answered.

"That's super!" Martha said. "Have you already started?"

"Not yet. I was supposed to start after your funeral, but I hope I'll be able to start a bit sooner," Thomas joked.

"Me too," Martha said. She rocked silently back and forth in the rocking chair and hesitantly shifted her gaze toward the Christmas tree and began sniffing.

"Mom, are you crying?" Elizabeth asked

Martha lifted her head and looked at her children through tear filled eyes. "I just can't believe this is happening," she said.

Everyone was silent as they waited for Martha to continue.

"I knew the cruise would be good for me and I thought it would be good for all of you as well. But I never dreamed that I'd return home to all of this." Martha took a hanky from her pocket and wiped her eyes before continuing. "For years I've been praying that somehow our family would become whole again. I have to confess that I was afraid it would take my death to accomplish that."

Everyone's eyes filled with tears as they listened.

"I'm just overwhelmed by everything that has

happened this past week. This is the best Christmas gift I have ever received. I may not be dead," Martha concluded, "but I'm surely in heaven."

Thomas got out of his chair and walked over to Martha. He took an envelope from his jacket pocket and placed it in her hand. "Then consider this a heavenward plea for forgiveness," he said.

"James gave you my letter, didn't he?" Martha asked Thomas.

Thomas nodded. "You can read that later, after you get home. And Dad was right," he added, "there's always tomorrow."

Martha reached up and gently placed her hand on Thomas' cheek. "I knew someday you'd understand."

"Look, I think we've all cried enough," Mary said after wiping her eyes. "Can't we talk about something a little less emotional?"

"That's a good idea. Anna, Joseph tells me his parents are spending Christmas in New Zealand. Why don't you tell him about your trip to New Zealand last summer?" Martha suggested.

Anna glared at Martha. "Mother!" she said through closed teeth.

"Actually, I'd like to hear about it," Joseph said.

"Go on, tell him," Rachel prodded.

"There's not enough time tonight," Anna responded.

"What about tomorrow?" Elizabeth asked.

"Tomorrow's Christmas," Anna replied, "not exactly the time to be talking about past vacations."

"Then what about the next day?" Mary inquired.

"I'll be at work on Tuesday," Anna said smugly.

"Don't you get a lunch break?" Rachel asked.

"Probably not, I have to be available to watch the showroom," Anna explained. Her face was turning red and she began to feel hot. "Anyway, shouldn't someone let the children know their grandmother is all right?"

Elizabeth looked at Mary and smiled. "I suppose someone should," she agreed.

"Then, if you'll excuse me for a minute, I'll go get them." Anna stood and quickly left the room.

"She's just a little shy," Martha said to Joseph.

"Well, maybe some other time," Joseph suggested. "Anyway, I'll be spending Tuesday teaching a customer how to use a new piece of equipment I sold him."

"What do you sell, anyway?" Thomas asked.

"Jeweler's equipment," Joseph replied.

Everyone in the room turned and stared at Joseph.

In an effort to hide his uneasiness, Joseph attempted to smile. "Did I say something wrong?" he sheepishly asked.

"On the contrary," Martha said with a grin. She winked at Elizabeth who had started to chuckle.

Everybody, except Joseph, began to laugh.

Joseph's discomfort increased as he gazed at the others. His half-hearted smile was replaced by an obvious look of confusion. "Am I missing something?" he asked as he shook his head.

"Right now perhaps," James teased, "but I think you'll understand later."

Before Joseph had a chance to respond, five screaming children came rushing into the front room to confirm the good news their Aunt Anna had brought them. "Grandma!" they all shouted in unison.

Once again, Martha began to cry. She pulled her grandchildren close to her and kissed each one on the cheek.

"Listen, unless there is something we can do to help with dinner," Martha said, "I propose we retire to the family room where we can enjoy the fire in the fireplace."

"Nope," Elizabeth replied, "I believe everything is under control. Dinner will be ready in about an hour."

Martha stood up and took two-year-old Samuel in her arms. "Come on everyone, let's celebrate Christmas the traditional Cooper way," she said.

The excited group followed Martha into the family room where Anna was sitting on the floor thumbing through a large Bible.

The children sat on the floor in a semicircle in front of the fireplace while Martha sat on the elevated stone hearth. The rest of the adults found comfortable seats behind the children. Martha asked Anna for the Bible.

Placing the large book on her lap, Martha opened to the second chapter of Luke in the New Testament and began reading, *"And it came to pass in those days..."*

About the Author

Todd F. Cope grew up in Spanish Fork, Utah, where he still resides. As the youngest of thirteen children, he quickly learned to get along with others. After graduating from high school, he served an LDS mission to Western Australia where he met a missionary from New Zealand who would later become his wife.

Todd and Denise were married in New Zealand and lived there for two years before returning to the United States so he could continue his education. He graduated from Utah Valley State College in Orem, Utah with an associate degree in nursing and later from Weber State University in Ogden, Utah with a baccalaureate degree in nursing. Most of his career has been spent in the Emergency Room. Currently he is the Director of Nursing at an assisted living center in Provo, Utah. He enjoys gardening, running, and spending time with his wife and four children.

Todd's love for writing dates back to the fourth grade when he won a poetry writing contest. He continued to be honored for his essays, poetry, and prose throughout his school career. Todd has published many articles on a variety of subjects in several forums including the *Ensign* and *New Era* magazines. He is the author of *The Shift*, a self-published novel that inspired the CBS Television movie *The Last Dance*, starring Maureen O'Hara.